The

Joy of Juicing

R E C I P E   G U I D E

CREATIVE COOKING WITH YOUR JUICER

Gary Null and

Shelly Null

Golden Health Publishing

New York

Golden Health Publishing is distributed to the trade by:

Book Mail Services
Golden Lee Book Distributors, Inc.
1000 Dean Street
Brooklyn, NY 11238

Publisher's Cataloging in Publication

Null, Gary.
    The joy of juicing recipe guide : creative cooking with your
juicer / Gary Null, Shelly Null.
    p. cm.
    Includes glossary and index.
    ISBN 0-912331-20-8

    1. Food processor cookery. 2. Blenders (Cookery). 3. Fruit
juices. 4. Vegetable juices. I. Null, Shelly. II. Title.
III. Title: Creative cooking with your juicer.

TX840.F6N8 1992

    641.589
    QBI92-10462

Printed in the United States of America by Paragon Press, Honesdale, PA.

10 9 8 7 6 5

Contents

*Dedicated to the people
who will be waking up
to juicing and renewed health.*

Acknowledgments

Special thanks go out to Katherine Farrell for her sincere dedication in seeing this project through. I'd like to thank Vicki Rollins for her artistic input. I would also like to acknowledge Lucy Alvarez and Kathy Davis for their persistence and editorial assistance.

Introduction

Today, millions of Americans are concerned about their health—and with good reason. According to various reports, we are overfed but undernourished. Our diets contain too many animal proteins, saturated fats, and chemically processed foods. Even worse, we spend billions of dollars each year on health care. Our medical bill for 1991 alone climbed to nearly $700 billion. Obviously, something is terribly wrong with our lifestyle.

Granted, no one silver bullet will correct this problem. It would be irresponsible to claim that you could make an isolated change—such as "juicing" more often, taking vitamins, or altering your diet—and achieve significant results. But we do know that you can feel a great deal better by making some changes in the quality of your life. These include exercising daily, reducing stress, cleaning up your home and work environments, and improving your diet, especially by including more meatless dishes and more foods that are high in vitamins and minerals, but low in calories and saturated fats.

The Art of Juicing

One excellent way to begin making healthy lifestyle changes is to include more juices in your diet. This book will teach you how to do so in a more comprehensive way than most other juicing books on the market have been able to do. When we decided to write a book on juicing, in fact, we realized that it would have to accomplish more than most of its predecessors did. We believe that many of the other juicing books have been written by people who don't truly understand nutritional requirements. As a result, the advice that's offered sometimes misses the mark. For instance, you cannot drink large quantities of dark green vegetable juices, because these powerful juices can cause an upset stomach. Nor can you drink straight carrot juice day after day. This juice has a high glucose content that will first raise your blood sugar level and then quickly drop it again. And, it's simply not reasonable to expect people to juice the same foods each day. Many juicing books also wrongly claim that you must drink juices within minutes of preparation, or they will no longer be good.

This book will help you to gauge the actual nutrient values of various fruit and vegetable juices made from produce in its natural (raw) form. Indeed, most fruits and vegetables should be juiced raw, since cooking can cause a substantial loss of nutrients. However, certain vegetables, such as broccoli, cauliflower, asparagus, and Brussels sprouts, should not be juiced in their natural state. They should instead be quickly steamed and then chilled in cold water before juicing.

This book also provides exciting, mouth-watering recipes for juices and for other dishes that include juice and the valuable pulp fiber among their ingredients. All ingredients can be easily obtained, and all recipes can be prepared with relative ease, regardless of whether you are sixteen or sixty years of age, are cooking for one or for a family of five, and are financially well off or living on a limited income.

With many of the recipes, we have tried to include a full spectrum of nutrients, including vitamins and minerals, essential amino acids, complex carbohydrates, and essential fatty acids. We also tested all recipes on segments of Gary's radio audience, and used audience feedback to perfect the recipes until we felt that they were as good as we could possibly make them.

Juices should be taken at least once a day, preferably in the morning, before you do any exercising. A glass of vegetable juice in the morning helps stimulate a natural energy process far superior to that created by a cup of coffee, which artificially jump-starts your adrenal glands and severely irritates the body's chemistry. Beyond that, juice can be taken one or two more times a day. You can take it to work in a thermos, give it to the kids, or use it in other dishes, such as soups, salads, appetizers, casseroles, and desserts.

Indeed, our Seven-Day Menu Plan (see page 175) shows that foods can be as creative as you want them to be while maintaining certain traditional tastes and aromas, as well as visual appeal. All of our dishes are based on people's general expectations regarding flavor. The difference is that these dishes are made with healthy foods. We believe that the fruits and vegetables used in these recipes should be organically grown, without sprays, whenever possible. It's no secret that we all have consumed thousands of man-made chemicals that have no place in our diets or our bodies. These chemicals can undermine our well-being.

Remember that the primary reason for drinking juices is to obtain vitamins, minerals, and chlorophyll. Proteins, complex carbohydrates, and essential fatty acids can be obtained from other foods, including grains, legumes, fish, nuts and seeds, and starchy vegetables. Fresh fruit juices are also rich in enzymes, which many nutritionists and health experts downplay or virtually overlook. We consider enzymes essential for well-being, and emphasize the exogenous variety— those that come from our foods—to promote proper digestion and biochemical processes.

The food values we've listed in our nutrient tables (see page 191) come from the latest edition of the United States Department of Agriculture (USDA) handbook. The average portion listed is 100 grams, or roughly 3 ounces. We have also listed the percentage of nutrients in a whole piece of fruit or vegetable and in a single slice. By using these tables, you will be able to easily determine the amounts of nutrients—primarily vitamins and minerals—you will obtain when you add several slices of produce, a whole item, or more to a glass of juice.

The Benefits of Protein Powder

A variety of protein powder mixes can be added to your juices and other foods as a means of enhancing the total nutrient value. Those protein powders found in health-food stores are usually the most wholesome, and commonly consist of rice, sesame seeds, egg whites, and soy blends, with high protein, complex-carbohydrate, and fiber contents, as well as essential vitamins and minerals.

Years ago, Gary created his own protein powder, Null-Trim, because he was losing too much lean muscle tisssue during long-distance training. Gary looked gaunt, and while he still had some strength from his body-building and weight-lifting days in college, he didn't have the speed he wanted.

Drawing on lessons learned in his earlier training days, Gary mixed protein derived from rice with a natural sweetener such as fruit juice to give himself at least 100 percent of the vitamins and minerals he needed. That way, he could go for a workout with an easily digestible, high-quality, low-calorie energy source. Now, Gary feels great and uses his protein drink before every workout. In the past year, he has continued to set American records, both indoors and outdoors, and has also won gold medals in national track and field competitions. And he still competes at an age when most people have become couch potatoes!

We recommend that you use protein powder once or twice a day in your juices or other foods. In addition, be sure to mix your sources of juice so that you eat both fruits and vegetables each day. Protein powder can be added to your juice and used as a mid-morning, mid-afternoon, or mid-evening snack. It also can be used to increase the protein value of any hot cereal, and can serve as a meal replacement, provided that you use two scoops. Those who travel will find it an easy way to improve the nutritional value of on-the-run meals.

Some of the finest athletes in America regularly mix protein powder with their juices. These athletes include Dave McGovern, a world-class athlete; Gary Morgan, a member of the Olympic team; Sam Skinner, a gold medalist in national track and field; Joan Roland and Louise Nottage, both of whom hold world records; and Auslug Thomas, Queenie Thompson, Thelma Wilson, Julie Ratner, and Franco Pentoni.

Again, we are not suggesting that any vitamin or mineral is curative on its own, but we are saying that these nutrients play a vital role in good nutrition. With this book, we want to alert everyone, from cynic to health advocate, of some strong evidence that's come to light in the mainstream scientific community. This evidence proves that diets which include wholesome foods that are rich in vitamins and minerals—of which juices are a primary example—can indeed play a role in maintaining optimum health.

The Need for Fundamental Change

In recent years, we have seen overwhelming evidence that the American diet must change if we are to improve our health. On October 22, 1991, United Press International reported, "The United States ranks at the bottom of a comparison of ten industrialized nations' health care systems."

Few people today can dispute the poor quality of the average American diet. As the *Los Angeles Times* Wire Service reported in September 1991, "Food is the ideal source of vitamins and minerals but many Americans don't eat a well-balanced diet. Some people believe they are too busy. Others are ill and have no appetite. And some individuals compromise nutrition by following ill-advised diets hoping to lose weight quickly."

The nutritional deficiencies that result from a poor diet lead to a long list of illnesses. Recent findings show that six of the ten leading causes of death in the United States are associated with diet, including heart disease, stroke, cancer, adult onset of diabetes, arteriosclerosis, and sclerosis of the liver.

Vitamin deficiencies, in particular, can lead to severe problems. Dr. Earl Dawson and colleagues at the University of Texas' Galveston medical branch, for example, studied people with dysplasia (which indicates abnormal cells in the cervix and may even be precancerous), and found that these patients had significantly lower levels of vitamins A and C than did people with normal cells. "Deficiencies of vitamin

A have been correlated with cancer of the bladder, breast, lungs and upper gastrointestinal tract," said Dr. Dawson in *Prevention* magazine.

Another recent study by Swiss scientists also showed that a lack of vitamins can increase the risk of cancer. In this study, researchers tracked 3,000 men for twelve years, and found that a lack of vitamin A and beta-carotene, in particular, was linked to an increased risk of lung cancer and increased deaths from all cancers, as reported in *The American Journal of Epidemiology*. Low levels of vitamin C were also found to heighten the risk of stomach and intestinal cancer.

In early 1990, the American Cancer Society began a program to increase public awareness of the diet's role in lowering the risks of certain cancers. Through its publication, *Cancer News,* the organization recommends that Americans choose foods that are rich in vitamins A and C, low in fat, and high in fiber. It also suggests the consumption of foods from the cruciferous family, which includes Brussels sprouts, cabbage, broccoli, cauliflower, kale, and turnips.

Indeed, many health advocates warn that our diets must be changed to minimize the intake of fats. According to the July 1990 issue of *Modern Medicine,* "A report released by the National Cholesterol Education Program recommends that all children and teenagers in the United States lower their cholesterol levels through dietary measures. The panel recommended that children eat foods low in saturated fats, total fats and cholesterol, and need a wide variety of foods to insure adequate intake of carbohydrates, protein and essential nutrients."

Recent evidence from a massive study spanning China, the United States, and Canada indicates that the more fat in the diet, the greater the risk of colon cancer. According to Dr. Alice Wittemore, the Stanford University Medical Center epidemiologist who headed the study, "We have been told not to eat saturated fats to avoid heart disease, but this is the first real evidence that they cause cancer." In 1988, doctors reported 152,000 new cases of colon cancer and 139,000 deaths from the disease in the United States, a per-person rate four to seven times higher than that of China, according to a report in the *Journal of the National Cancer Institute.*

One of the most comprehensive studies ever conducted on the link between diet and disease began in 1983 and included 65,000 Chinese people. The study was completed in 1991, with the results being published in a 928-page volume by Cornell University. The study compared the diets of Chinese and American people, and concluded that the Chinese consume 20 percent more calories than Americans— but that Americans eat 25 percent more fat. As reported in *The New England Journal of Medicine,* the study showed that a diet high in complex carbohydrates, similar to the one recommended in this cookbook, was linked to a significant improvement in overall health and a reduced incidence of various diseases.

The differences between the Chinese and American diets are indeed substantial. In the November 1991 issue of the *Medical Tribune,* T. Colin Campbell, Ph.D., of Cornell University said, "Seventy percent of the protein intake in the United States is from animal foods. In China, that figure is 7 percent. It is an enormous difference."

Meanwhile, researchers at St. Luke's Roosevelt Hospital in New York found that people who reduced the amount of saturated fats in their diets to a total caloric intake of less than 25 percent, doubled their natural killer cell immune effectiveness. In 1989, a study published in *Nutrition Research* concluded that certain types of fats, particularly saturated fats, can increase the incidence of cancerous tumors.

As the evidence supporting dietary change continues to grow, the "basic four food groups" on which most Americans were raised have gone the way of the Edsel. Previously, meat and dairy products were the centerpiece of the American diet, while grains, fruits, and vegetables were of secondary importance. Now, doctors and nutritionists sponsored by the Committee for Responsible Medicine have reshuffled the four food groups so that meat and dairy are merely "optional." The emphasis has clearly shifted to grains, legumes, vegetables, and fruits. In fact, the new regime has advised us to have three or more servings each of vegetables and fruits a day.

This change in food consciousness now extends beyond core health-food enthusiasts and into the general public. Safeway and Raley, two large supermarkets in northern California, now carry organic produce. More than half of the stores' customers eat a great deal of produce on a regular basis, and 45 percent of the supermarkets now feature salad bars. Lucky Stores, California's largest supermarket chain, is considering stocking organic produce. And, according to the 1989 issue of *Longevity* magazine, fast-food chains now offer more vegetable dishes, lower-fat burgers, and healthier cooking oils.

Those who make fundamental changes in diet will benefit substantially from the consumption of more disease-preventing nutrients. Vitamins C and E, for example, can help the body prevent immunological disorders—especially damage to the arteries—and can even help reverse various degrees of heart disease. Similarly, research conducted by Dr. Douglas Heimburger at the University of Alabama Medical Center, Birmingham, found that folic acid, contained in green leafy vegetables, and vitamin B_{12} may serve as primary preventive measures against cancer.

In a 533-page book on the importance of vitamins, the New York Academy of Sciences illustrated that vitamin E alone can help to decrease the incidence of cancer and protect against premature aging. This nutrient also decreases the inflammation of arthritis and increases immune system functioning, primarily by serving as an antioxidant and a scavenger of free radicals, substances known to cause cell damage.

Other reports show that vitamin C helps to lower blood pressure. This connection was noted in a study that analyzed the vitamin C levels of the blood of 241 elderly Chinese Americans. The more vitamin C, the lower the blood pressure. And virtually all of the vitamin C came from food, according to researchers from the U.S. Department of Agriculture's Human Nutrition Research Center on Aging and Tuft's University. According to *Choice* magazine, this same link was found in another study of 67 people of all ages who had normal to mildly high blood pressure.

Senior citizens, who tend to eat poorly, often suffer from inordinate levels of diet-related disease. A report by the American Heart Association reprinted in the April 1990 issue of *Modern Medicine* states, "More than one half of American women over age 55 have cholesterol levels of 240 or more, increasing their risk of heart disease and stroke." And, according to an article in the October 1990 issue of *Geriatric Medicine Today,* "Plasma and leukocyte concentrations have been shown to decline with age, perhaps because of a variety of factors, such as a change in diet."

A growing number of Americans are overweight for their age, according to the August/September 1991 issue of the *Townsend Letter.* Today, some 64 percent of Americans fall into this category, said Mark Brickland, editor of *Prevention* magazine, which commissioned a study on the subject. In 1983, 58 percent of the magazine's respondents were overweight for their age.

Again, the solution to this problem must begin with a change in attitude. The November 1991 issue of the *Medical Tribune* said: "Overweight, sedentary people have more misconceptions and negative attitudes about food than those of ideal weight who are physically active. These issues are important because Americans will not change their eating habits until their attitudes change, according to nutritional researchers."

The studies discussed above merely confirm what numerous other scientific reports and clinical observations have also shown: The better a person's diet, the better his or her overall health and well-being. The worse the diet and the more serious the nutritional deficiencies, the worse his or her well-being.

It takes motivation, discipline, and a desire to be well to make the dietary changes that will eventually make a difference in your life. If you make one small change but continue other destructive behavior, you won't compensate for the negative impact of your lifestyle. You can't negate smoking with vitamin C, unrelenting stress with B complex, or a diet that's high in saturated fats with a little fiber. However, when fundamental changes *are* made and are incorporated into our daily lives, improved health is sure to follow, giving us ample rewards for our efforts.

The Basics of Juicing

You'll find that juicing not only is fun, but also is an easy way to make delicious, healthful drinks and boost the flavor and nutritional value of many of your favorite dishes. When using your juicer, you'll want to follow the manufacturer's directions for best results. In addition, the following guidelines, which apply to *most* juicers, will help you to use the recipes in this book and will insure success when you create your own special recipes.

☐ When possible, use organically grown produce—produce that's cultivated without the use of harmful chemicals.

☐ Whenever you're unable to get organically grown produce, remove the peel, as this is where most of the chemical residues can be found. Waxed fruits and vegetables should always be peeled before juicing, as the wax is difficult to remove.

☐ When produce is being juiced with the peel intact, wash the produce well by holding it under running water and scrubbing it with a vegetable brush. (A vegetable brush is also a wonderful means of quickly cleaning the stainless steel strainer found in most juicers.)

☐ The skins of most fruits and vegetables may be left on. Some skins, however, should be removed, either because they are too thick or because they are known to contain toxic substances. Those fruits that should be peeled before juicing include pineapples, kiwis, papayas, oranges, and grapefruits.

☐ All seeds should be removed from fruits before juicing. Some seeds—apple seeds, for instance—actually contain toxic substances. Many other seeds will impart an unpleasant bitter taste to the juice. Naturally, all pits *must* be removed before the produce is juiced.

☐ Most fruits and vegetables should be juiced raw, as cooking will deplete stores of vitamins, minerals, and enzymes. However, certain vegetables—broccoli, cauliflower, asparagus, Brussels sprouts, and potatoes—should *not* be juiced raw. Before juicing these vegetables, steam them briefly, and then chill them.

☐ Whenever a recipe calls for mashed bananas, you can easily use your juicer to mash the bananas for you. Simply peel the desired number of bananas, place them in the freezer, and, when frozen, "juice" them! The resulting "pulp" will be creamy and lumpless.

☐ Because of their hard consistency, nuts cannot be fed through the juicer. Whenever recipes call for ground nuts, use a blender, food processor, or food mill to grind the nuts to the desired consistency. When preparing shakes and other drinks that include nuts, simply toss the whole or halved nuts into the blender or food processor with the other ingredients. Two or three minutes of blending should produce a smooth, creamy beverage. Remember that whenever ground nuts are called for, an equal amount of nut butter can be substituted.

☐ To add extra nutrients to juices and other dishes, add a scoop or two of protein powder to boost protein, complex-carbohydrate, fiber, and vitamin and mineral contents. Used as a supplement to a balanced diet of vegetables, fruits, and grains, protein powder will help insure that you receive all the nutrients you need for good health.

A Word About Measurements

All of the recipes in *The Joy of Juicing* list both the amount of juice or pulp used in that particular recipe, *and* the amount of fruit or vegetables that will most likely yield the desired quantities of juice or pulp. The following conversion table—which lists the juice yield of *medium-sized* fruits and vegetables— will help you as you prepare these and other juicing recipes. Keep in mind, though, that the amount of juice derived from, say, one apple will depend not only on the size and variety of the apple, but also on your juicer. For this reason, the conversion table should be viewed only as a guideline. As you use your juicer, you'll learn whether more or less produce is usually needed to yield the required amount of juice.

JUICE CONVERSION TABLE

Produce	¼ Cup Juice	½ Cup Juice	1 Cup Juice
Apple	1 piece	2 pieces	4 pieces
Beet	1 piece	2 pieces	4 pieces
Cabbage	¼ piece	½ piece	1 piece
Carrot	1 piece	2 pieces	4 pieces
Cauliflower	¼ piece	½ piece	1 piece

Produce	¼ Cup Juice	½ Cup Juice	1 Cup Juice
Celery	1 piece	2 pieces	4 pieces
Cherry	½ cup	1 cup	2 cups
Cranberry	1 cup	2 cups	4 cups
Cucumber	½ piece	1 piece	2 pieces
Honeydew Melon	¾ cup	1½ cups	3 cups
Kiwi	1 piece	2 pieces	4 pieces
Leek	1 piece	2 pieces	4 pieces
Lemon	2 pieces	4 pieces	8 pieces
Mango	½ piece	1 piece	2 pieces
Nectarine	¾ piece	1½ pieces	3 pieces
Orange	1 piece	2 pieces	4 pieces
Papaya	½ piece	1 piece	2 pieces
Parsnip	5 pieces	10 pieces	20 pieces
Peach	¾ piece	1½ pieces	3 pieces
Pear	1 piece	2 pieces	4 pieces
Pepper, Green	3 pieces	6 pieces	12 pieces
Pepper, Red	3 pieces	6 pieces	12 pieces
Pineapple	¼ piece	½ piece	1 piece
Plum	1½ pieces	3 pieces	6 pieces
Potato, Sweet	½ piece	1 piece	2 pieces
Potato, White	½ piece	1 piece	2 pieces
Squash, Acorn	½ piece	1 piece	2 pieces
Squash, Butternut	¼ piece	½ piece	1 piece
Squash, Yellow	1 piece	2 pieces	4 pieces
Strawberry	2 cups	4 cups	8 cups
Tangerine	1 piece	2 pieces	4 pieces
Tomato	½ piece	1 piece	2 pieces
Watermelon	¾ cup	1½ cups	3 cups
Zucchini	1 piece	2 pieces	4 pieces

Juices, Shakes, and Drinks

CARROT PEAR JUICE

6 pears (1½ cups juice)
3 carrots (¾ cup juice)
2 bananas, mashed
1½ cups ice

1. Separately juice the pears and carrots. Set aside 1½ cups of the pear juice and ¾ cup of the carrot juice.
2. In a blender or food processor, combine the juices with the bananas and ice, and blend for 2 minutes, or until smooth.
3. Serve immediately.

Makes 3½ cups.

ZOWIE MAUI JUICE

1 tangerine ($\frac{1}{4}$ cup juice)
1 kiwi ($\frac{1}{4}$ cup juice)
$\frac{1}{4}$ pineapple ($\frac{1}{4}$ cup juice)
$\frac{3}{4}$ cup ice

1. Separately juice the tangerine, kiwi, and pineapple. Set aside $\frac{1}{4}$ cup of the tangerine juice, $\frac{1}{4}$ cup of the kiwi juice, and $\frac{1}{4}$ cup of the pineapple juice.

2. In a blender or food processor, combine the juices with the ice, and blend for 2 minutes, or until smooth.

3. Serve immediately.

Makes 1$\frac{1}{2}$ cups.

GINGERY APPLE JUICE

6 apples (1$\frac{1}{2}$ cups juice)
1 beet ($\frac{1}{4}$ cup juice)
1 small piece ginger root
(1 teaspoon juice)

1. Separately juice the apples, beet, and ginger. Set aside 1½ cups of the apple juice, ¼ cup of the beet juice, and 1 teaspoon of the ginger juice.

2. Combine the juices, and serve immediately.

Makes 1¾ cups.

CITRUS TONIC

4 oranges (1 cup juice)
½ grapefruit (⅓ cup juice)
1 lemon (2 tablespoons juice)
½ cup club soda
1 cup ice

1. Separately juice the oranges, grapefruit, and lemon. Set aside 1 cup of the orange juice, ⅓ cup of the grapefruit juice, and 2 tablespoons of the lemon juice.

2. In a blender or food processor, combine the juices with the club soda and ice, and blend for 2 minutes, or until smooth.

3. Serve immediately.

Makes 2½ cups.

APPLE SPROUT JUICE

6 apples (1½ cups juice)
4 carrots (1 cup juice)
½ cup sunflower or alfalfa sprouts
(1 tablespoon juice)

1. Separately juice the apples, carrots, and sprouts. Set aside 1½ cups of the apple juice, 1 cup of the carrot juice, and 1 tablespoon of the sprout juice.

2. Combine the juices, and serve immediately.

Makes 2½ cups.

CELERY APPLE JUICE

4 stalks celery (1 cup juice)
4 apples (1 cup juice)
4 carrots (1 cup juice)

1. Separately juice the celery, apples, and carrots. Set aside 1 cup of the celery juice, 1 cup of the apple juice, and 1 cup of the carrot juice.

2. Combine the juices, and serve immediately.

Makes 3 cups.

LEMON CUCUMBER JUICE

2 cucumbers (1 cup juice)

2 apples ($\frac{1}{2}$ cup juice)

1 yellow squash ($\frac{1}{4}$ cup juice)

$\frac{1}{2}$ zucchini (2 tablespoons juice)

1$\frac{1}{2}$ green bell peppers
(2 tablespoons juice)

1 teaspoon pure lemon extract

1 cup ice

1. Separately juice the cucumbers, apples, yellow squash, zucchini, and green peppers. Set aside 1 cup of the cucumber juice, $\frac{1}{2}$ cup of the apple juice, $\frac{1}{4}$ cup of the yellow squash juice, 2 tablespoons of the zucchini juice, and 2 tablespoons of the green pepper juice.

2. In a blender or food processor, combine the juices with the lemon extract and ice, and blend for 2 minutes, or until smooth.

3. Serve immediately.

Makes 3 cups.

APPLE CARROT JUICE

4 apples (1 cup juice)
4 carrots (1 cup juice)
small bunch fresh parsley
(1 tablespoon juice)
1 cup ice

1. Separately juice the apples, carrots, and parsley. Set aside 1 cup of the apple juice, 1 cup of the carrot juice, and 1 tablespoon of the parsley juice.

2. In a blender or food processor, combine the juices with the ice, and blend for 2 minutes, or until smooth.

3. Serve immediately.

Makes 2½ cups.

PEACHY CHERRY JUICE

6 apples (1½ cups juice)
3 peaches (1 cup juice)
¼ cup frozen pitted cherries
1 cup ice

1. Separately juice the apples and peaches. Set aside 1½ cups of the apple juice and 1 cup of the peach juice.

2. In a blender or food processor, combine the juices with the remaining ingredients, and blend for 2 minutes, or until smooth.

3. Serve immediately.

Makes 3½ cups.

REFRESHING
WATERCRESS JUICE

4 apples (1 cup juice)
2 stalks celery (½ cup juice)
1 beet (¼ cup juice)
1 small bunch watercress (1 tablespoon juice)
½ lemon (1 tablespoon juice)

1. Separately juice the apples, celery, beet, watercress, and lemon. Set aside 1 cup of the apple juice, ½ cup of the celery juice, ¼ cup of the beet juice, 1 tablespoon of the watercress juice, and 1 tablespoon of the lemon juice.

2. Combine the juices, and serve immediately.

Makes 1¾ cups.

BANANA STRAWBERRY JUICE

2 apples (¹⁄₂ cup juice)
1 pear (¹⁄₄ cup juice)
2 cups strawberries (¹⁄₄ cup juice)
2 stalks celery (¹⁄₂ cup juice) or ¹⁄₂ cup water
¹⁄₂ banana, mashed
1 cup ice

1. Separately juice the apples, pear, strawberries, and celery (if desired). Set aside ½ cup of the apple juice, ¼ cup of the pear juice, ¼ cup of the strawberry juice, and ½ cup of the celery juice.

2. In a blender or food processor, combine the juices with the banana and ice, and blend for 2 minutes, or until smooth. If you've chosen not to use celery juice, add ½ cup of water instead.

3. Serve immediately.

Makes 2¹⁄₂ cups.

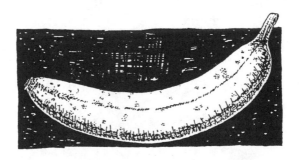

BEET GREENS VEGETABLE JUICE

2 apples ($^{1}/_{2}$ cup juice)
2 carrots ($^{1}/_{2}$ cup juice)
1 small bunch beet greens (1 tablespoon juice)
1 beet ($^{1}/_{4}$ cup juice)
1$^{1}/_{2}$ cups ice

1. Separately juice the apples, carrots, beet greens, and beet. Set aside ½ cup of the apple juice, ½ cup of the carrot juice, 1 tablespoon of the beet greens juice, and ¼ cup of the beet juice.

2. In a blender or food processor, combine the juices with the ice, and blend for 2 minutes, or until smooth.

3. Serve immediately.

Makes 2$^{1}/_{4}$ cups.

ORANGE GINGER JUICE

6 oranges (1½ cups juice)

*1 small piece ginger root
(1 teaspoon juice)*

¼ cup cranberries (1 tablespoon juice)

1 cup ice

1. Separately juice the oranges, ginger, and cranberries. Set aside 1½ cups of the orange juice, 1 teaspoon of the ginger juice, and 1 tablespoon of the cranberry juice.

2. In a blender or food processor, combine the juices with the ice, and blend for 2 minutes, or until smooth.

3. Serve immediately.

Makes 2 cups.

SWISS CHARD CELERY JUICE

4 carrots (1 cup juice)

2 apples (½ cup juice)

½ cucumber (¼ cup juice)

1 stalk celery (¼ cup juice)

1 small bunch Swiss chard (1 tablespoon juice)

1. Separately juice the carrots, apples, cucumber, celery, and Swiss chard. Set aside 1 cup of the carrot juice, ½ cup of the apple juice, ¼ cup of the cucumber juice, ¼ cup of the celery juice, and 1 tablespoon of the Swiss chard juice.

2. Combine the juices, and serve immediately.

Makes 2 cups.

TANGY PURPLE CABBAGE SURPRISE

2 stalks celery (½ cup juice)
½ head purple cabbage (½ cup juice)
2 apples (½ cup juice)
1 beet (¼ cup juice)
½ lemon (1 tablespoon juice)

1. Separately juice the celery, cabbage, apples, beet, and lemon. Set aside ½ cup of the celery juice, ½ cup of the cabbage juice, ½ cup of the apple juice, ¼ cup of the beet juice, and 1 tablespoon of the lemon juice.

2. Combine the juices, and serve immediately.

Makes 1¾ cups.

CAULIFLOWER BEET JUICE

3 stalks celery ($^3/_4$ cup juice)

2 carrots ($^1/_2$ cup juice)

$^1/_4$ head cauliflower, steamed and chilled
($^1/_4$ cup juice)

1 beet ($^1/_4$ cup juice)

1 small piece ginger root
(1 teaspoon juice)

1. Separately juice the celery, carrots, cauliflower, beet, and ginger. Set aside $^3/_4$ cup of the celery juice, $^1/_2$ cup of the carrot juice, $^1/_4$ cup of the cauliflower juice, $^1/_4$ cup of the beet juice, and 1 teaspoon of the ginger juice.

2. Combine the juices, and serve immediately.

Makes $1^3/_4$ cups.

CRANBERRY GINGER TONIC

4 carrots (1 cup juice)

4 pears (1 cup juice)

$^1/_4$ cup cranberries (1 tablespoon juice)

1 small piece ginger root
(1 teaspoon juice)

1. Separately juice the carrots, pears, cranberries, and ginger. Set aside 1 cup of the carrot juice, 1 cup of the pear juice, 1 tablespoon of the cranberry juice, and 1 teaspoon of the ginger juice.

2. Combine the juices, and serve immediately.

Makes 2 cups.

CHERRY PLUM SURPRISE

5 apples (1¼ cups juice)
3 plums (½ cup juice)
1 lemon (2 tablespoons juice)
¼ cup frozen pitted cherries
1 cup ice

1. Separately juice the apples, plums, and lemon. Set aside 1¼ cups of the apple juice, ½ cup of the plum juice, and 2 tablespoons of the lemon juice.

2. In a blender or food processor, combine the juices with the cherries and ice, and blend for 2 minutes, or until smooth.

3. Serve immediately.

Makes 3 cups.

LEMON KIWI SPRITZER

4 cups peeled watermelon chunks
(1⅓ cups juice)
3 carrots (⅔ cup juice)
3 kiwis (⅔ cup juice)
1 lemon (2 tablespoons juice)
1⅓ cups ice

1. Separately juice the watermelon, carrots, kiwis, and lemon. Set aside 1⅓ cups of the watermelon juice, ⅔ cup of the carrot juice, ⅔ cup of the kiwi juice, and 2 tablespoons of the lemon juice.

2. In a blender or food processor, combine the juices with the ice, and blend for 2 minutes, or until smooth.

3. Serve immediately.

Makes 3½ cups.

ROMAINE LEMON TONIC

6 apples (1½ cups juice)
2 carrots (½ cup juice)
3–4 leaves romaine lettuce (¼ cup juice)
½ lemon (1 tablespoon juice)

1. Separately juice the apples, carrots, lettuce, and lemon. Set aside 1 ½ cups of the apple juice, ½ cup of the carrot juice, ¼ cup of the lettuce juice, and 1 tablespoon of the lemon juice.

2. Combine the juices, and serve immediately.

Makes 2¼ cups.

CRANBERRY
PINEAPPLE COCKTAIL

1 pineapple (1 cup juice)
2 cups peeled watermelon chunks (⅔ cup juice)
½ cup cranberries (2 tablespoons juice)
1 lemon (2 tablespoons juice)
⅔ cup seltzer
½ cup ice

1. Separately juice the pineapple, watermelon, cranberries, and lemon. Set aside 1 cup of the pineapple juice, ⅔ cup of the watermelon juice, 2 tablespoons of the cranberry juice, and 2 tablespoons of the lemon juice.

2. In a blender or food processor, combine the juices with the seltzer and ice, and blend for 2 minutes, or until smooth.

3. Serve immediately.

Makes 3 cups.

ICED CINNAMON AND SPICE TEA

2 apples ($\frac{1}{2}$ cup juice)
1 orange (3 tablespoons juice)
1 Bengal Spice tea bag (Celestial Seasonings)
1 cup boiling water
$\frac{1}{4}$ teaspoon ground cinnamon
1 cup ice

1. Separately juice the apples and orange. Set aside $\frac{1}{2}$ cup of the apple juice and 3 tablespoons of the orange juice.

2. Steep the tea bag in the boiling water for 4–6 minutes. Discard the tea bag, and set aside the tea.

3. In a blender or food processor, combine the juices with the tea, cinnamon, and ice, and blend for 2 minutes, or until smooth.

4. Serve immediately.

Makes 2$\frac{1}{2}$ cups.

WATERMELON SPRITZER

2 cups peeled watermelon chunks (²⁄₃ cup juice)
²⁄₃ pineapple (²⁄₃ cup juice)
½ cup seltzer
¾ cup ice

1. Separately juice the watermelon and pineapple. Set aside ²⁄₃ cup of the watermelon juice and ²⁄₃ cup of the pineapple juice.

2. In a blender or food processor, combine the juices with the seltzer and ice, and blend for 2 minutes, or until smooth.

3. Serve immediately.

Makes 2¾ cups.

SUPER PEACHY SHAKE

3 peaches (1 cup juice)

4 apples (1 cup juice)

1 banana, mashed

*1 tablespoon ground or whole unsalted
almonds or almond butter*

1 tablespoon unsweetened flaked coconut

½ cup unsweetened soymilk

1½ cups ice

1. Separately juice the peaches and apples. Set aside 1 cup of the peach juice and 1 cup of the apple juice.

2. In a blender or food processor, combine the juices with the remaining ingredients, and blend for 2 minutes, or until smooth.

3. Serve immediately.

Makes 4 cups.

GRANDMA'S MIXED VEGETABLE JUICE

2 apples ($\frac{1}{2}$ cup juice)
2 pears ($\frac{1}{2}$ cup juice)
2 carrots ($\frac{1}{2}$ cup juice)
1 cucumber ($\frac{1}{2}$ cup juice)
1 beet ($\frac{1}{4}$ cup juice)
1 small bunch Swiss chard (1 tablespoon juice)
1 red bell pepper (1 tablespoon juice)
1 small piece ginger root
(1 teaspoon juice)

1. Separately juice the apples, pears, carrots, cucumber, beet, Swiss chard, red pepper, and ginger. Set aside ½ cup of the apple juice, ½ cup of the pear juice, ½ cup of the carrot juice, ½ cup of the cucumber juice, ¼ cup of the beet juice, 1 tablespoon of the Swiss chard juice, 1 tablespoon of the red pepper juice, and 1 teaspoon of the ginger juice.

2. Combine the juices, and serve immediately.

Makes 2$\frac{1}{4}$ cups.

FROZEN AVOCADO SHAKE

1 apple (¼ cup juice)
¼ cup mashed avocado
¼ banana, mashed
½ cup fresh or frozen strawberries
½ cup unsweetened soymilk
½ teaspoon pure almond extract
1 cup ice

1. Juice the apple. Set aside ¼ cup of the juice.

2. In a blender or food processor, combine the apple juice with the remaining ingredients, and blend for 2 minutes, or until smooth.

3. Serve immediately.

Makes 2½ cups.

NECTARINE SHAKE

3 nectarines (1 cup juice)
1 orange (3 tablespoons juice)
¼ cup frozen strawberries
1½ cups unsweetened soymilk

1. Separately juice the nectarines and orange. Set aside 1 cup of the nectarine juice and 3 tablespoons of the orange juice.

2. In a blender or food processor, combine the juices with the strawberries and soymilk, and blend for 2 minutes, or until smooth.

3. Serve immediately.

Makes 2¾ cups.

ALMOND COCONUT SHAKE

1 papaya (½ cup juice)

2 tablespoons unsweetened flaked coconut

2 tablespoons unsalted hulled sunflower seeds

3 tablespoons protein powder
(optional, see pages 4–5)

1 teaspoon pure almond extract

½ cup seltzer

1 cup ice

1. Juice the papaya. Set aside ½ cup of the juice.

2. In a blender or food processor, combine the juice with the remaining ingredients, and blend for 2 minutes, or until smooth.

3. Serve immediately.

Makes 2¼ cups.

CARROT BANANA SHAKE

2 apples ($\frac{1}{2}$ cup juice)

1 carrot ($\frac{1}{4}$ cup juice)

$\frac{1}{2}$ banana, mashed

1 teaspoon unsweetened flaked coconut

*1 teaspoon ground or whole unsalted almonds
or almond butter*

dash of pure almond extract

$\frac{1}{2}$ cup ice

1. Separately juice the apples and carrot. Set aside ½ cup of the apple juice and ¼ cup of the carrot juice.

2. In a blender or food processor, combine the juices with the remaining ingredients, and blend for 2 minutes, or until smooth.

3. Serve immediately.

Makes 1$\frac{1}{4}$ cups.

STRAWBERRY ALMOND SHAKE

4 apples (1 cup juice)

1 banana, mashed

½ cup fresh or frozen strawberries

¼ cup ground or whole unsalted almonds or almond butter

1 tablespoon pure unsweetened cocoa powder (unsweetened carob powder may be substituted)

1¼ cups ice

1. Juice the apples. Set aside 1 cup of the juice.
2. In a blender or food processor, combine the juice with the remaining ingredients, and blend for 2 minutes, or until smooth.
3. Serve immediately.

Makes 3 cups.

HONEYDEW MELON SHAKE

2 cups peeled honeydew melon chunks
($^2/_3$ cup juice)

1 banana, mashed

1 tablespoon unsweetened flaked coconut

2 tablespoons ground or whole unsalted
almonds or almond butter

1 tablespoon chopped dates

$^1/_2$ cup unsweetened soymilk

$^1/_2$ teaspoon pure almond extract

$^3/_4$ cup ice

1. Juice the melon. Set aside $^2/_3$ cup of the juice.

2. In a blender or food processor, combine the juice
   with the remaining ingredients, and blend for 2
   minutes, or until smooth.

3. Serve immediately.

Makes 2 cups.

VERY NUTTY SHAKE

3 apples (¾ cup juice)

½ banana, mashed

2 tablespoons ground or whole unsalted
peanuts or peanut butter

¼ cup plus 2 tablespoons plain yogurt

1 tablespoon light-colored honey
(clover, tupelo, or wildflower)

1 tablespoon pure unsweetened cocoa powder
(unsweetened carob powder may be
substituted)

½ teaspoon pure vanilla extract

1 cup ice

1. Juice the apples. Set aside ¾ cup of the juice.

2. In a blender or food processor, combine the juice
   with the remaining ingredients, and blend for 2
   minutes, or until smooth.

3. Serve immediately.

Makes 2 cups.

PECAN SHAKE

1 apple (¼ cup juice)

¼ banana, mashed

*⅓ cup ground or whole unsalted pecans
or pecan butter*

*3 tablespoons protein powder
(optional, see pages 4–5)*

½ teaspoon pure lemon extract

1 cup seltzer

1 cup ice

1. Juice the apple. Set aside ¼ cup of the juice.

2. In a blender or food processor, combine the juice with the remaining ingredients, and blend for 2 minutes, or until smooth.

3. Serve immediately.

Makes 2½ cups.

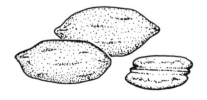

APPLE
STRAWBERRY SHAKE

2 apples (½ cup juice)

1 banana, mashed

3 tablespoons ground or whole unsalted pecans
or pecan butter

¼ cup fresh or frozen strawberries

½ cup unsweetened soymilk

¼ teaspoon pure lemon extract

½ cup ice

1. Juice the apples. Set aside ½ cup of the juice.

2. In a blender or food processor, combine the juice with the remaining ingredients, and blend for 2 minutes, or until smooth.

3. Serve immediately.

Makes 1¾ cups.

CHOCOLATE WALNUT SHAKE

4 apples (1 cup juice)

2 bananas, mashed

4 tablespoons ground or whole unsalted
walnuts or walnut butter

1 cup unsweetened soymilk

1½ tablespoons pure unsweetened
cocoa powder (unsweetened carob powder
may be substituted)

1 teaspoon pure almond extract

1 cup ice

1. Juice the apples. Set aside 1 cup of the juice.

2. In a blender or food processor, combine the juice
   with the remaining ingredients, and blend for 2
   minutes, or until smooth.

3. Serve immediately.

Makes 3 cups.

CREAMY BANANA YOGURT SHAKE

4 apples (1 cup juice)
3 bananas, mashed
½ cup chopped dates
2 tablespoons unsweetened flaked coconut
½ cup plain yogurt
½ teaspoon pure almond extract
½ teaspoon ground nutmeg
2 cups ice

1. Juice the apples. Set aside 1 cup of the juice.

2. In a blender or food processor, combine the juice with the remaining ingredients, and blend for 2 minutes, or until smooth.

3. Serve immediately.

Makes 3½ cups.

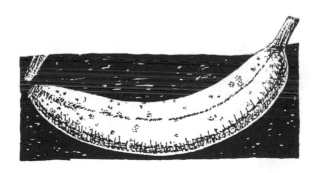

BLUEBERRY MACADAMIA SHAKE

2 pears ($\frac{1}{2}$ cup juice)
$\frac{1}{2}$ cup blueberries
$\frac{1}{4}$ cup ground or whole unsalted
macadamia nuts
1 banana, mashed
$\frac{3}{4}$ cup unsweetened soymilk
$\frac{1}{2}$ teaspoon pure lemon extract
1 cup ice

1. Juice the pears. Set aside $\frac{1}{2}$ cup of the juice.

2. In a blender or food processor, combine the juice with the remaining ingredients, and blend for 2 minutes, or until smooth.

3. Serve immediately.

Makes 3 cups.

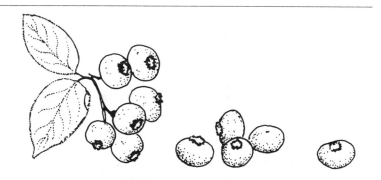

TANGY SWEET CARROT SHAKE

3 carrots (²⁄₃ cup juice)
2 apples (½ cup juice)
½ cup cranberries (2 tablespoons juice)
1 cup fresh or frozen strawberries
½ cup plain yogurt
1 teaspoon ground nutmeg
1 cup ice

1. Separately juice the carrots, apples, and cranberries. Set aside ²⁄₃ cup of the carrot juice, ½ cup of the apple juice, and 2 tablespoons of the cranberry juice.

2. In a blender or food processor, combine the juices with the remaining ingredients, and blend for 2 minutes, or until smooth.

3. Serve immediately.

Makes 3 cups.

CHERRY COCONUT SHAKE

2 cups peeled honeydew melon chunks
($\frac{2}{3}$ cup juice)

1 banana, mashed

$\frac{1}{4}$ cup frozen pitted cherries

1 tablespoon unsweetened flaked coconut

2 tablespoons unsalted ground or whole
almonds or almond butter

$\frac{1}{2}$ cup unsweetened soymilk

1 cup ice

1. Juice the melon. Set aside $\frac{2}{3}$ cup of the juice.

2. In a blender or food processor, combine the juice with the remaining ingredients, and blend for 2 minutes, or until smooth.

3. Serve immediately.

Makes $2\frac{1}{2}$ cups.

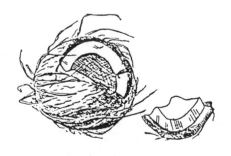

PINEAPPLE DATE SHAKE

¾ pineapple (¾ cup juice)

2 tablespoons chopped dates

1 tablespoon unsweetened flaked coconut

*1 tablespoon ground or whole unsalted pecans
or pecan butter*

¼ cup plain yogurt

½ teaspoon ground nutmeg

1 cup ice

1. Juice the pineapple. Set aside ¾ cup of the juice.

2. In a blender or food processor, combine the juice with the remaining ingredients, and blend for 2 minutes, or until smooth.

3. Serve immediately.

Makes 2 cups.

CREAMY
WATERMELON SHAKE

3 cups peeled watermelon chunks (1 cup juice)
1 banana, mashed
¼ cup plain yogurt
½ teaspoon pure almond extract
½ teaspoon ground cinnamon
1 cup ice

1. Juice the watermelon. Set aside 1 cup of the juice.

2. In a blender or food processor, combine the juice with the remaining ingredients, and blend for 2 minutes, or until smooth.

3. Serve immediately.

Makes 2¼ cups.

CREAMY CAROB SHAKE

2 apples ($\frac{1}{2}$ cup juice)

1 banana, mashed

1 tablespoon unsalted hulled sunflower seeds

$\frac{1}{2}$ cup unsweetened soymilk

*2 teaspoons unsweetened carob powder
(pure unsweetened cocoa powder
may be substituted)*

*3 tablespoons protein powder
(optional, see pages 4–5)*

1 teaspoon pure maple syrup

$\frac{1}{2}$ teaspoon pure vanilla extract

$\frac{1}{4}$ teaspoon pure almond extract

$\frac{1}{2}$ teaspoon ground cinnamon

1 cup ice

1. Juice the apples. Set aside $\frac{1}{2}$ cup of the juice.

2. In a blender or food processor, combine the juice with the remaining ingredients, and blend for 2 minutes, or until smooth.

3. Serve immediately.

Makes 2 cups.

ORANGE CAROB SHAKE

1–2 oranges (⅓ cup juice)

1 tangerine (¼ cup juice)

¼ banana, mashed

1 tablespoon ground or whole unsalted walnuts
or walnut butter

¾ cup unsweetened soymilk

1 tablespoon unsweetened carob powder
(pure unsweetened cocoa powder
may be substituted)

½ teaspoon pure vanilla extract

¼ teaspoon ground cinnamon

1 cup ice

1. Separately juice the orange and tangerine. Set aside ⅓ cup of the orange juice and ¼ cup of the tangerine juice.

2. In a blender or food processor, combine the juices with the remaining ingredients, and blend for 2 minutes, or until smooth.

3. Serve immediately.

Makes 2½ cups.

TROPICAL
PINEAPPLE SHAKE

1 apple ($\frac{1}{4}$ cup juice)

1 slice pineapple (2 tablespoons juice)

1 slice papaya (1 tablespoon juice)

$\frac{1}{2}$ lemon (1 teaspoon juice)

$\frac{1}{4}$ cup mashed avocado

$\frac{1}{2}$ cup seltzer

$\frac{1}{8}$ teaspoon pure lemon extract

$\frac{1}{8}$ teaspoon ground nutmeg

1 cup ice

1. Separately juice the apple, pineapple, papaya, and lemon. Set aside $\frac{1}{4}$ cup of the apple juice, 2 tablespoons of the pineapple juice, 1 tablespoon of the papaya juice, and 1 teaspoon of the lemon juice.

2. In a blender or food processor, combine the juices with the remaining ingredients, and blend for 2 minutes, or until smooth.

3. Serve immediately.

Makes 2$\frac{1}{4}$ cups.

PAPAYA LIME SHAKE

1 apple (¼ cup juice)
1 slice papaya (1 tablespoon juice)
½ lemon (1 tablespoon juice)
½ lime (1 teaspoon juice)
½ cup seltzer
⅛ teaspoon pure lemon extract
⅛ teaspoon ground nutmeg
1 cup ice

1. Separately juice the apple, papaya, lemon, and lime. Set aside ¼ cup of the apple juice, 1 tablespoon of the papaya juice, 1 tablespoon of the lemon juice, and 1 teaspoon of the lime juice.

2. In a blender or food processor, combine the juices with the remaining ingredients, and blend for 2 minutes, or until smooth.

3. Serve immediately.

Makes 2 cups.

Breakfast Foods

TROPICAL MILLET DELIGHT

6 apples (1½ cups juice)

1 cup water

½ cup millet

¼ cup mashed banana

2 tablespoons chopped dates

1 tablespoon unsweetened flaked coconut

½ teaspoon pure almond extract

1. Juice the apples. Set aside 1½ cups of the juice.

2. In a large saucepan, combine the water and apple juice, and bring to a boil over high heat.

3. Reduce the heat to medium-low, and stir in the millet. Cook uncovered until the water is absorbed, about 10 minutes.

4. Add the remaining ingredients, and stir.

5. Serve hot with unsweetened soymilk or juice.

Serves 2.

WESTERN OMELET

1 cup mushrooms (¼ cup pulp)
1 green bell pepper (⅛ cup pulp)
½ yellow onion (2 tablespoons pulp)
3 eggs, beaten
1 tablespoon sweet butter

1. Separately juice the mushrooms, green pepper, and onion. Set aside ¼ cup of the mushroom pulp, ⅛ cup of the pepper pulp, and 2 tablespoons of the onion pulp.

2. In a medium-sized mixing bowl, combine the eggs with the mushroom, pepper, and onion pulp.

3. Heat the butter in a large frying pan. Pour the egg mixture into the frying pan, and cook over medium heat for 3–4 minutes, or until the eggs solidify.

4. Fold the omelet over, and serve hot with whole grain bread.

Serves 1.

BARLEY CEREAL WITH APPLES AND SPICE

4 oranges (1 cup juice)
2 apples (½ cup pulp)
½ cup water
⅓ cup pearl barley
⅓ cup whole dried apricots
3 tablespoons pure maple syrup
½ teaspoon ground cinnamon

1. Separately juice the oranges and the apples. Set aside 1 cup of the orange juice and ½ cup of the apple pulp.

2. In a medium-sized saucepan, combine the orange juice and water, and bring to a boil over high heat.

3. Reduce the heat to medium-low, and stir in the barley. Cook uncovered for 10–15 minutes, stirring occasionally.

4. Add the apple pulp and the remaining ingredients, and cook for an additional 5–10 minutes, stirring occasionally.

5. Serve hot with unsweetened soymilk or juice.

Serves 2.

COCOA KASHA WITH BANANAS

4 apples (1 cup juice)

1 cup water

½ cup unsweetened soymilk

⅓ cup kasha

½ cup mashed banana

*½ tablespoon pure unsweetened cocoa powder
(unsweetened carob powder may be
substituted)*

¼ cup pure maple syrup

dash of ground cinnamon

1. Juice the apples. Set aside 1 cup of the juice.

2. In a medium-sized saucepan, combine the apple juice, water, and soymilk, and bring to a boil over high heat.

3. Reduce the heat to medium-low, and stir in the kasha. Cook uncovered for 3–4 minutes, stirring occasionally.

4. Add the remaining ingredients, and cook for an additional 3–4 minutes, stirring occasionally.

5. Serve hot with unsweetened soymilk or juice.

Serves 2.

CREAM OF RICE WITH PEACHES AND HONEY

3 peaches ($^{3}/_{4}$ cup pulp)

1$^{1}/_{2}$ cups water

1 cup unsweetened soymilk

$^{1}/_{3}$ cup cream of brown rice cereal or farina

*2 tablespoons light-colored honey
(clover, tupelo, or wildflower)*

$^{1}/_{2}$ cup chopped dates

$^{1}/_{2}$ teaspoon pure almond extract

dash of ground nutmeg

1. Juice the peaches. Set aside $^{3}/_{4}$ cup of the pulp.

2. In a medium-sized saucepan, combine the water and soymilk, and bring to a boil over high heat.

3. Reduce the heat to medium-low, and stir in the cream of brown rice or farina. Cook uncovered for 3–4 minutes, stirring occasionally.

4. Add the peach pulp and the remaining ingredients, and cook for an additional 3–4 minutes, stirring occasionally.

5. Serve hot with unsweetened soymilk or juice.

Serves 2.

CARROT SUNFLOWER GRANOLA

2 carrots ($\frac{1}{2}$ cup pulp)

1 cup rolled oats

$\frac{1}{2}$ cup whole unsalted almonds

$\frac{1}{4}$ cup raisins

$\frac{1}{4}$ cup unsalted hulled sunflower seeds

$\frac{1}{2}$ cup pure maple syrup

2 teaspoons pure almond extract

$\frac{1}{2}$ teaspoon ground cinnamon

1. Preheat the oven to 375°F.

2. Juice the carrots. Set aside $\frac{1}{2}$ cup of the pulp.

3. In a large mixing bowl, combine the carrot pulp with the remaining ingredients, mixing well.

4. Spread the mixture on a greased cookie sheet, and bake for 15 minutes, or until the top of the mixture turns brown.

5. Serve hot over ice cream or cold with unsweetened soymilk.

Serves 2.

HEARTY OATS WITH NUTS AND RAISINS

4 pears (1 cup juice)
1 cup water
1 cup rolled oats
1 banana, sliced
¼ cup raisins
¼ cup chopped unsalted black walnuts
½ teaspoon pure vanilla extract
dash of ground cinnamon

1. Juice the pears. Set aside 1 cup of the juice.
2. In a medium-sized saucepan, combine the water and pear juice, and bring to a boil over high heat.
3. Reduce the heat to medium-low, and stir in the oats. Cook uncovered for 5 minutes, stirring occasionally.
4. Add the remaining ingredients, and cook for an additional 5 minutes, stirring occasionally.
5. Serve hot with unsweetened soymilk.

Serves 2.

SWEET
RICE CREAM CEREAL

4 apples (1 cup juice and 2 tablespoons pulp)
½–¾ cup water
1½ cups unsweetened soymilk
½ cup short-grain brown rice
¼ cup raisins
¼ cup unsalted chopped pecans
2 tablespoons light-colored honey
(clover, tupelo, or wildflower)
½ teaspoon pure vanilla extract
¼ teaspoon ground cinnamon

1. Juice the apples. Set aside 1 cup of the juice and 2 tablespoons of the pulp.

2. In a large saucepan, combine the apple juice, water, and soymilk, and bring to a boil over high heat.

3. Reduce the heat to low, and stir in the rice. Cover, and continue cooking until the water is absorbed, about 30 minutes.

4. Add the apple pulp and the remaining ingredients, and stir.

5. Serve hot with unsweetened soymilk or juice.

Serves 2.

BANANA PECAN PANCAKES

6 apples (1½ cups juice)

1 carrot (¼ cup pulp)

2 eggs, beaten

¼ cup pure maple syrup

½ cup water

1 cup whole wheat flour

2 teaspoons baking powder

½ cup toasted wheat germ

½ cup sliced bananas

¼ cup unsalted pecans, halved or chopped

2 tablespoons raisins

⅓ teaspoon ground cinnamon

2 tablespoons cold-pressed flavorless oil
(sunflower, safflower, or canola)

1. Separately juice the apples and the carrot. Set aside 1½ cups of the apple juice and ¼ cup of the carrot pulp.

2. In a large mixing bowl, combine the apple juice, eggs, maple syrup, and water, mixing well.

3. Stir in the flour, baking powder, and wheat germ, mixing well.

4. Stir in the carrot pulp, bananas, pecans, raisins, and cinnamon.

5. For each pancake, heat 1 tablespoon of oil in a small (6- or 8-inch) frying pan over medium heat. When the oil is hot, pour half the batter into the frying pan so that the bottom of the pan is covered with batter. Let the pancake cook for 2–3 minutes, or until the underside is brown.

6. Flip the pancake over, and reduce the heat to low. Cut the pancake into 8 wedges to allow the center to cook. Cook for an additional 2 minutes, or until the center is done.

7. Serve hot with unsweetened soymilk or juice.

Serves 2.

Soups

VEGETABLE MILLET SOUP

1 recipe Classic Vegetable Stock (see page 72)

2 cups water

½ zucchini, chopped

¼ cup chopped celery

¼ cup chopped carrots

⅛ cup millet

1. In a medium-sized saucepan, combine the stock with the water, and bring to a boil over high heat.

2. Reduce the heat to medium-low, add the remaining ingredients, and simmer uncovered for 10 minutes.

3. Serve hot with whole grain bread.

Serves 2.

GINGERY BEAN SOUP

2 acorn squash (1 cup juice and ½ cup pulp)

1 small piece ginger root
(1 teaspoon juice)

2¾–3 cups water

1 cup chopped tomatoes

¼ cup cooked white beans

1 tablespoon chopped fresh cilantro

¼ teaspoon sea salt

⅛ teaspoon black pepper

1. Separately juice the squash and ginger. Set aside 1 cup of the squash juice, ½ cup of the squash pulp, and 1 teaspoon of the ginger juice.

2. In a medium-sized saucepan, combine the juices and pulp with the remaining ingredients, and bring to a boil over high heat. Reduce the heat to medium-low, and simmer uncovered for 5–10 minutes.

3. Serve hot with whole grain bread.

Serves 2.

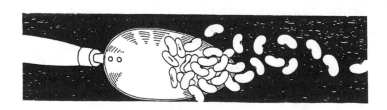

MUSHROOM BARLEY SOUP

8 stalks celery (2 cups juice)

1 cup sliced leeks

2 tablespoons extra virgin olive oil

5½ cups water

2 cups sliced mushrooms

1 cup chopped zucchini

½ cup pearl barley

1½ tablespoons chopped fresh dill

1½ teaspoons sea salt

1 teaspoon black pepper

2 sprigs fresh dill, as garnish

1. Juice the celery. Set aside 2 cups of the juice.
2. In a large saucepan, sauté the leeks in the oil until soft.
3. Add the juice, water, mushrooms, zucchini, barley, dill, salt, and pepper, and bring to a boil over high heat. Reduce the heat to medium-low, and simmer uncovered for 25–35 minutes, or until the barley is done.
4. Serve hot, garnished with the dill sprigs.

Serves 2.

CELERY POTATO SOUP

1 potato, steamed and chilled
(½ cup juice and ½ tablespoon pulp)

2 stalks celery (½ cup juice)

¼ cup chopped leeks

½ cup cubed potatoes

1 tablespoon cold-pressed flavorless oil
(sunflower, safflower, or canola)

1¼ cups unsweetened soymilk

½ teaspoon finely chopped fresh dill

1 teaspoon finely chopped fresh parsley

¼ teaspoon celery seeds

½–¾ teaspoon sea salt

¼–½ teaspoon black pepper

2 sprigs fresh dill, as garnish

1. Separately juice the potato and celery. Set aside ½ cup of the potato juice, ½ tablespoon of the potato pulp, and ½ cup of the celery juice.

2. In a large saucepan, sauté the leeks and potato cubes in the oil for 3–4 minutes.

3. Add the juices, pulp, soymilk, dill, parsley, celery seeds, salt, and pepper, and bring to a boil over high heat. Reduce the heat to medium-low, and simmer uncovered for 10 minutes, or until the potatoes are tender.

4. Serve hot, garnished with the dill sprigs.

Serves 2.

CREAMY TOMATO SOUP

1 butternut squash ($\frac{1}{2}$ cup pulp)
$\frac{1}{2}$ tomato ($\frac{1}{4}$ cup juice)
$\frac{1}{4}$ cup plus 3 tablespoons plain yogurt
$\frac{3}{4}$ cup chopped tomatoes
2 teaspoons chopped fresh dill
$\frac{1}{4}$ teaspoon sea salt
$\frac{1}{4}$ teaspoon black pepper
2 tablespoons plain yogurt, as garnish
2 tablespoons Parmesan cheese, as garnish
2 sprigs fresh dill, as garnish

1. Separately juice the squash and tomato. Set aside $\frac{1}{2}$ cup of the squash pulp and $\frac{1}{4}$ cup of the tomato juice.

2. In a medium-sized saucepan, combine the pulp, juice, and yogurt. Bring to a simmer over medium-low heat, and cook uncovered for 10–15 minutes.

3. Add the chopped tomato, dill, salt, and pepper, and remove from the heat.

4. Serve hot or cold, garnished with the yogurt, Parmesan cheese, and dill sprigs.

Serves 2.

ORIENTAL
MISO VEGETABLE SOUP

1 leek (¼ cup juice)
3 carrots (¾ cup juice)
2 tablespoons brown rice miso
4 cups water
½ cup destemmed shiitake mushrooms
1 cup diced extra firm tofu
¼ cup snow pea pods
¼ cup cubed squash (any type), unpeeled
1 tablespoon toasted (dark) sesame oil
1 tablespoon chopped scallions
1 teaspoon chopped garlic
1 teaspoon chopped fresh cilantro
½ teaspoon grated ginger root
½ teaspoon diced red chili peppers
½ teaspoon hot (spicy) sesame oil

1. Separately juice the leek and carrots. Set aside ¼ cup of the leek juice and ¾ cup of the carrot juice.

2. In a large saucepan, dissolve the miso in the water and stir well.

3. Add the juices and remaining ingredients, and bring to a boil over high heat. Reduce the heat to medium-low, and simmer uncovered for 15–20 minutes.

4. Serve hot with whole grain bread.

Serves 2.

PAPAYA SQUASH SOUP

2–3 acorn squash
(1¼ cups juice and ½ cup pulp)
2 papaya (1 cup juice)
2½–3 cups water
½ teaspoon ground nutmeg
¼ cup papaya slices, as garnish
¼ cup halved seedless red grapes
or pomegranate seeds, as garnish

1. Separately juice the squash and papaya. Set aside 1¼ cups of the squash juice, ½ cup of the squash pulp, and 1 cup of the papaya juice.

2. In a medium-sized saucepan, combine the juices, pulp, water, and nutmeg, and bring to a boil over high heat. Reduce the heat to medium-low, and simmer uncovered for 5–7 minutes.

3. Serve hot or cold, garnished with the papaya slices and red grapes.

Serves 2.

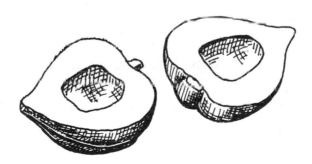

Classic Vegetable Stock

1 carrot (¼ cup juice, plus pulp)

1 stalk celery (¼ cup juice, plus pulp)

3 green bell peppers (¼ cup juice, plus pulp)

1¼ cups water

¼ cup chopped yellow onions

1 clove garlic, crushed

1 tablespoon extra virgin olive oil

1 teaspoon chopped fresh thyme
or ½ teaspoon dried thyme

½ teaspoon celery seeds

1 bay leaf

1 teaspoon sea salt

½ teaspoon black pepper

1. Separately juice the carrot, celery, and green peppers. Set aside ¼ cup each of the carrot, celery, and green pepper juice. Combine the carrot, celery, and green pepper pulps, and set aside ½ cup.

2. In a medium-sized saucepan, combine the juices and pulp with the remaining ingredients, and bring to a boil over high heat. Reduce the heat to medium-low, and simmer uncovered for 15 minutes.

3. Strain the soup stock through a fine colander or cheesecloth, collecting the liquid.

4. Serve hot as is, or use as a base for other soups.

Serves 1.

SOUTHWESTERN SQUASH SOUP

1 butternut squash (1 cup juice)

¼ cup cooked black beans

¼ cup water

2 tablespoons plain yogurt

½ cup chopped tomatoes

*1 teaspoon chopped fresh basil
or ½ teaspoon dried basil*

½ teaspoon finely chopped jalapeño peppers

½ teaspoon finely chopped fresh cilantro

2 tablespoons plain yogurt, as garnish

2 tablespoons chopped tomatoes, as garnish

2 sprigs fresh cilantro, as garnish

1. Juice the squash. Set aside 1 cup of the juice.

2. In a blender or food processor, combine the black beans with the water, and blend until you have a smooth purée. Set aside ½ cup of the purée.

3. In a medium-sized saucepan, combine the squash juice, black bean purée, and yogurt. Mix thoroughly with a whisk until creamy.

4. Add the tomato, basil, jalapeño pepper, and chopped cilantro, and simmer uncovered over medium-low heat for 5–10 minutes.

5. Serve hot or cold, garnished with the yogurt, tomatoes, and cilantro sprigs.

Serves 2.

CINNAMON FRUIT SOUP

1 butternut squash (½ cup juice and ¾ cup pulp)
2 pears (½ cup juice)
1½ cups unsweetened soymilk
1 teaspoon pure vanilla extract
¾ teaspoon ground cinnamon
6 slices orange, as garnish
2 sprigs fresh mint, as garnish

1. Separately juice the squash and pears. Set aside ½ cup of the squash juice, ¾ cup of the squash pulp, and ½ cup of the pear juice.

2. In a medium-sized saucepan, combine the juices, pulp, soymilk, vanilla extract, and cinnamon, and bring to a boil over high heat. Reduce the heat to medium-low, and simmer uncovered for 4–6 minutes.

3. Serve hot or cold, garnished with the orange slices and mint sprigs.

Serves 2.

CHILLED
CUCUMBER MINT SOUP

2 cucumbers (1 cup juice)
4 stalks celery (1 cup juice)
1 cup plain yogurt
½ cup chopped peeled cucumbers
2 teaspoons finely chopped fresh mint
2 teaspoons chopped fresh parsley
¼ cup diced red bell pepper or pomegranate
seeds, as garnish
2 sprigs fresh mint, as garnish

1. Separately juice the cucumbers and celery. Set aside 1 cup of the cucumber juice and 1 cup of the celery juice.

2. In a medium-sized mixing bowl, combine the juices, yogurt, cucumber, mint, and parsley. Blend with a whisk until creamy. Chill for one hour.

3. Serve cold, garnished with the diced red pepper and mint sprigs.

Serves 2.

PASTA AND WHITE BEAN SOUP

3 cucumbers (1½ cups juice)
½ head cauliflower, steamed and chilled
(½ cup pulp)
¼ cup diced yellow onions
3 tablespoons extra virgin olive oil
¾ cup water
1½ cups chopped tomatoes
¾ cup cooked white beans
½ cup chopped escarole or kale
¼ cup chopped celery
¼ cup sliced carrots
¼ cup uncooked whole grain macaroni
2 teaspoons chopped fresh parsley
2 teaspoons chopped fresh basil
½ teaspoon sea salt
½ teaspoon black pepper
1 clove garlic, crushed

1. Separately juice the cucumbers and cauliflower. Set aside 1½ cups of the cucumber juice and ½ cup of the cauliflower pulp.

2. In a large saucepan, sauté the onion in the oil for 2–3 minutes.

3. Add the cucumber juice and water, and bring to a boil over high heat. Reduce the heat to medium-

low, add the remaining ingredients, and simmer uncovered for 15 minutes, or until the pasta is tender.

4. Serve hot or cold with bread.

Serves 2 to 4.

Salads

CURRIED WALDORF SALAD

$\frac{1}{2}$ lemon (1 tablespoon juice)

2 cups diced unpeeled apples

2 cups diced unpeeled pears

1 cup diced celery

1 cup unsalted walnut halves

$\frac{1}{2}$ cup raisins

$\frac{1}{2}$ cup Curry Mayonnaise (see page 108)

1. Juice the lemon. Set aside 1 tablespoon of the juice.
2. In a medium-sized mixing bowl, combine the lemon juice with the remaining ingredients, and mix well.
3. Serve cold or at room temperature.

Serves 2.

TOMATO GARLIC PASTA SALAD

*4 cups cooked whole grain pasta
(bow ties, shells, or ziti)*

3 cups Tomato Salsa (see page 109)

2 cups steamed broccoli florets

1 cup whole pine nuts

1. In a large mixing bowl, toss the pasta with the remaining ingredients.

2. Serve cold as a main dish or a salad.

Serves 2.

MIXED DARK GREEN SALAD

2 beets ($\frac{1}{2}$ cup pulp)

1 cup chopped radicchio

1 cup chopped Belgian endive

1 cup chopped arugula

1 cup chopped Swiss chard

1 cup unsalted walnut halves

1 recipe Dijon Salad Dressing (see page 81)

1. Juice the beets. Set aside ½ cup of the pulp.
2. In a large mixing bowl, toss the beet pulp with the radicchio, endive, arugula, Swiss chard, and walnuts.
3. Toss the salad with the desired amount of Dijon Salad Dressing, and serve cold or at room temperature with whole grain bread.

Serves 2.

Dijon Salad Dressing

¾ cup cold-pressed flavorless oil
(sunflower, safflower, or canola)

6 tablespoons water

3 tablespoons prepared Dijon mustard

3 tablespoons apple cider vinegar

1 teaspoon finely chopped fresh herbs
(chives, basil, and/or parsley)

¼ teaspoon sea salt

¼ teaspoon black pepper

1. In a small mixing bowl, combine all the ingredients, and mix well with a fork or whisk.
2. Serve over salads.

Makes 1 cup.

ZESTY
TUNA SALAD

1 carrot ($\frac{1}{4}$ cup pulp)

1 lemon (2 tablespoons juice)

13 ounces canned or cooked fresh tuna

4–5 tablespoons Basic Mayonnaise
(see page 106)

$\frac{1}{4}$ cup unsalted hulled sunflower seeds

$\frac{1}{4}$ cup chopped celery

$\frac{1}{2}$ teaspoon sea salt

$\frac{1}{4}$ teaspoon black pepper

1. Separately juice the carrot and lemon. Set aside $\frac{1}{4}$ cup of the carrot pulp and 2 tablespoons of the lemon juice.

2. In a medium-sized mixing bowl, flake the tuna with a fork.

3. Add the carrot pulp, lemon juice, and Basic Mayonnaise, and mix.

4. Add the remaining ingredients, and mix.

5. Serve cold over salad greens or as a sandwich filling.

Serves 2–3.

CUCUMBER RAITA SALAD

½ cucumber (¼ cup juice)
2 cups plain yogurt
1 tablespoon chopped fresh cilantro
2 teaspoons ground cardamom
½ cup chopped peeled cucumbers
½ cup chopped tomatoes

1. Juice the cucumber. Set aside ¼ cup of the juice.

2. In a small mixing bowl, combine the cucumber juice with the yogurt, and mix well with a whisk.

3. Stir in the cilantro and cardamom, and mix.

4. Add the chopped cucumbers and tomatoes, and mix.

5. Serve cold or at room temperature with bread or almost any main dish. This salad goes especially well with Matar Paneer (see page 122).

Serves 2.

CAESAR SALAD WITH THYME CROUTONS

3 carrots (¾ cup pulp)
4½ cups chopped romaine lettuce
¼ cup Dijon Salad Dressing (see below)
¾ cup Thyme Croutons (see page 85)
1½ tablespoons grated Parmesan cheese

1. Juice the carrots. Set aside ¾ cup of the pulp.

2. In a large mixing bowl, toss the carrot pulp with the lettuce.

3. Toss the salad with the desired amount of Dijon Salad Dressing, Thyme Croutons, and Parmesan cheese, and serve cold or at room temperature.

Serves 2.

Dijon Salad Dressing

¾ cup cold-pressed flavorless oil
(sunflower, safflower, or canola)
6 tablespoons water
3 tablespoons prepared Dijon mustard
3 tablespoons apple cider vinegar

1 teaspoon finely chopped fresh herbs
(chives, basil, and/or parsley)

¼ teaspoon sea salt

¼ teaspoon black pepper

1. In a small mixing bowl, combine all the ingredients, and mix well with a fork or whisk.
2. Serve over salads.

Makes 1 cup.

Thyme Croutons

1 cup whole grain ¾-inch bread cubes

2–4 tablespoons extra virgin olive oil

1½ tablespoons finely chopped fresh thyme

dash of sea salt

1. Preheat the oven to 375°F.
2. In a small mixing bowl, combine all the ingredients and toss.
3. Spread the cubes on an ungreased cookie sheet and bake for 15–20 minutes, or until light brown in color.
4. Toss with salads.

Makes 1 cup.

GREEN BEAN SALAD WITH ALMONDS AND DILL

2 cups steamed green beans
¼ cup Dill Mayonnaise (see page 107)
¼ cup slivered blanched almonds
1 tablespoon poppy seeds
¼ cup sprigs fresh dill, as garnish

1. In a medium-sized mixing bowl, toss the beans with the Dill Mayonnaise.

2. Sprinkle the almonds and poppy seeds on top of the bean mixture.

3. Serve cold or at room temperature, garnished with the dill sprigs.

Serves 1.

TABOULI SALAD

3 cups bulghur wheat

1 cup boiling water

3 carrots ($^{3}/_{4}$ cup pulp)

2 lemons ($^{1}/_{4}$ cup juice)

$^{1}/_{2}$ cup raisins

$^{1}/_{2}$ cup finely chopped fresh parsley

$^{1}/_{2}$ cup chopped unsalted cashews

$^{1}/_{4}$ cup sliced scallions

2–3 tablespoons tamari soy sauce

1. In a large mixing bowl, pour the boiling water over the bulghur wheat. Cover the bowl with a towel, and let it stand for 30 minutes. Drain off any excess liquid.

2. Separately juice the carrots and lemons. Set aside $^{3}/_{4}$ cup of the carrot pulp and $^{1}/_{4}$ cup of the lemon juice.

3. In a large mixing bowl, combine the carrot pulp, lemon juice, and bulghur wheat with the remaining ingredients. Mix well, and drain off any excess liquid.

4. Serve cold or at room temperature with whole grain bread.

Serves 2.

RED POTATO SALAD

½ carrot
(1 tablespoon juice and 2 tablespoons pulp)
2 cups diced steamed red potatoes
½ cup chopped celery
2 tablespoons chopped red onions
2 tablespoons extra virgin olive oil
2 teaspoons chopped fresh dill
1 teaspoon celery seeds
1 teaspoon sea salt
½ teaspoon black pepper
⅛–¼ cup Basic Mayonnaise (see page 106)

1. Juice the carrot. Set aside 1 tablespoon of the juice and 2 tablespoons of the pulp.

2. In a medium-sized mixing bowl, toss the carrot juice and pulp with the remaining ingredients.

3. Serve cold or at room temperature.

Serves 2.

MIXED
SPROUT SALAD

2 beets ($\frac{1}{2}$ cup pulp)
2 cups lentil sprouts
1 cup radish sprouts
1 cup alfalfa sprouts
1 cup sliced red bell peppers
1 recipe Sesame Orange Dressing
(see page 93)

1. Juice the beets. Set aside ½ cup of the pulp.

2. In a large mixing bowl, toss the beet pulp with the sprouts and peppers.

3. Toss the salad with the desired amount of Sesame Orange Dressing, and serve at room temperature.

Serves 2.

COLESLAW
WITH FRESH DILL

1 carrot ($\frac{1}{4}$ cup pulp)
2 lemons (3 tablespoons juice)
2 cups shredded green cabbage
3 tablespoons Basic Mayonnaise (see page 106)
$\frac{1}{2}$ teaspoon prepared mustard
1 tablespoon chopped fresh dill
$\frac{1}{2}$ teaspoon sea salt
$\frac{1}{4}$ teaspoon black pepper
dash of apple cider vinegar

1. Separately juice the carrot and lemons. Set aside $\frac{1}{4}$ cup of the carrot pulp and 3 tablespoons of the lemon juice.

2. In a medium-sized mixing bowl, toss the carrot pulp and lemon juice with the remaining ingredients.

3. Serve cold as a salad or a sandwich filling.

Serves 2.

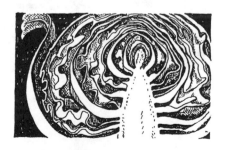

SUMMER FRUIT SALAD

$\frac{1}{2}$ *apple (2 teaspoons juice)*
$\frac{1}{2}$ *lemon (1$\frac{1}{2}$ teaspoons juice)*
1 cup diced peeled peaches
$\frac{1}{2}$ *cup blueberries*
$\frac{1}{2}$ *cup strawberries*
$\frac{1}{2}$ *cup raspberries*
$\frac{1}{2}$ *teaspoon pure almond extract*

1. Separately juice the apple and lemon. Set aside 2 teaspoons of the apple juice and 1 $\frac{1}{2}$ teaspoons of the lemon juice.

2. In a medium-sized mixing bowl, combine the juices with the remaining ingredients, and mix well.

3. Serve cold.

Serves 2.

Dressings, Sauces, Dips, and Spreads

SESAME ORANGE DRESSING

3 oranges (³⁄₄ cup juice)
¹⁄₄ cup toasted (dark) sesame oil
3 tablespoons sesame seeds
2 tablespoons hot (spicy) sesame oil

1. Juice the oranges. Set aside ³⁄₄ cup of the juice.

2. In a small mixing bowl, combine the orange juice with the remaining ingredients, and mix well.

3. Serve cold or at room temperature over salads.

Makes 1¹⁄₄ cups.

TOMATO SALAD DRESSING

1 tomato ($\frac{1}{2}$ cup juice)

2 lemons (3 tablespoons juice)

$\frac{1}{2}$ cup extra virgin olive oil

*1 teaspoon chopped fresh basil
or $\frac{1}{2}$ teaspoon dried basil*

*$\frac{1}{2}$ teaspoon chopped fresh oregano
or $\frac{1}{4}$ teaspoon dried oregano*

1 clove garlic, crushed

1. Separately juice the tomato and lemons. Set aside $\frac{1}{2}$ cup of the tomato juice and 3 tablespoons of the lemon juice.

2. In a blender or food processor, combine the juices with the remaining ingredients, and blend for 2 minutes, or until smooth.

3. Serve at room temperature over salads.

Makes 1$\frac{1}{4}$ cups.

SUNFLOWER SALAD DRESSING

2 lemons ($\frac{1}{4}$ cup juice)

$\frac{1}{4}$ cup unsalted hulled sunflower seeds

$\frac{1}{2}$ cup extra virgin olive oil

$\frac{1}{2}$ cup soft tofu

1–2 tablespoons water

1 tablespoon tamari soy sauce

*1 teaspoon chopped fresh basil
or $\frac{1}{2}$ teaspoon dried basil*

*1 teaspoon chopped fresh thyme
or $\frac{1}{2}$ teaspoon dried thyme*

1. Juice the lemons. Set aside $\frac{1}{4}$ cup of the juice.

2. Grind the sunflower seeds in a food mill or food processor. Set aside 1 cup of the ground seeds.

3. In a blender or food processor, combine the lemon juice and ground sunflower seeds with the remaining ingredients, and blend for 2 minutes, or until smooth.

4. Serve cold over salads or with raw vegetables.

Makes 1$\frac{1}{4}$ cups.

CILANTRO MINT DRESSING

4 lemons (½ cup juice)

1 cup finely chopped fresh cilantro

3 tablespoons water

*1½ tablespoons finely chopped
fresh mint*

*1½ teaspoons finely chopped
green chili peppers*

1. Juice the lemons. Set aside ½ cup of the juice.

2. In a small mixing bowl, combine the lemon juice with the remaining ingredients, and mix well.

3. Serve cold over salads. This dressing is especially good with Cucumber Raita Salad (see page 83) and unleavened bread.

Makes 1½ cups.

TAHINI
GARBANZO BEAN DRESSING

2 lemons (3 tablespoons juice)
⅞ cup cooked garbanzo beans (chickpeas)
⅛ cup water
¼ cup sesame tahini
1 clove garlic, crushed
¼ teaspoon sea salt

1. Juice the lemons. Set aside 3 tablespoons of the juice.

2. In a blender or food processor, combine the garbanzo beans and water, and blend until you have a smooth purée. Set aside 1 cup of the purée.

3. In a small mixing bowl, combine the lemon juice and garbanzo bean purée with the remaining ingredients, and blend with a whisk until smooth.

4. Serve at room temperature over salads, vegetables, brown rice, or whole grain pasta.

Makes 1¼ cups.

ZESTY TOMATO SAUCE

2 tomatoes (1 cup juice)
¼ cup chopped green bell peppers
2 tablespoons chopped yellow onions
¼ cup extra virgin olive oil
2½ cups chopped tomatoes
1 tablespoon tomato paste
1 tablespoon finely chopped fresh basil
1 clove garlic, crushed
½ teaspoon sea salt
½ teaspoon black pepper

1. Juice the 2 tomatoes. Set aside 1 cup of the juice.

2. In a medium-sized saucepan, sauté the green pepper and onion in the oil for 5 minutes.

3. Add the tomato juice and the remaining ingredients, and simmer over medium-low heat for 15–20 minutes.

4. Serve hot over whole grain pasta.

Makes 4 cups.

CILANTRO PESTO SAUCE

1 large bunch fresh parsley
(¾ cup pulp, plus juice)

1 small bunch fresh cilantro
(¼ cup pulp, plus juice)

2 tablespoons ground or whole unsalted
walnuts or walnut butter

½ cup extra virgin olive oil

1 clove garlic, minced

½ teaspoon sea salt

½ teaspoon black pepper

1. Separately juice the parsley and cilantro. Set aside ¾ cup of the parsley pulp and ¼ cup of the cilantro pulp. Combine the parsley and cilantro juices, and set aside 1 tablespoon.

2. In a blender or food processor, combine the parsley pulp, cilantro pulp, and mixed juices with the remaining ingredients, and blend for 2 minutes, or until smooth.

3. Serve at room temperature over vegetables or whole grain pasta.

Makes 1 cup.

CURRIED
ORANGE SAUCE

1 orange (¼ cup juice)
⅞ cup cooked garbanzo beans (chickpeas)
⅛ cup water
1 teaspoon curry powder
¼ teaspoon sea salt

1. Juice the orange. Set aside ¼ cup of the juice.

2. In a blender or food processor, combine the garbanzo beans and water, and blend until you have a smooth purée. Set aside 1 cup of the purée.

3. In a small mixing bowl, combine the orange juice and garbanzo bean purée with the remaining ingredients, and blend with a whisk until smooth.

4. Serve hot or cold over vegetables, brown rice, or whole grain pasta.

Makes 1¼ cups.

WALNUT PESTO SAUCE

1 large bunch fresh parsley
($\frac{3}{4}$ cup pulp, plus juice)

1 small bunch fresh basil
($\frac{1}{4}$ cup pulp, plus juice)

2 tablespoons ground or whole unsalted
walnuts or walnut butter

$\frac{1}{2}$ cup extra virgin olive oil

1 clove garlic, minced

$\frac{1}{2}$ teaspoon sea salt

$\frac{1}{2}$ teaspoon black pepper

1. Separately juice the parsley and basil. Set aside $\frac{3}{4}$ cup of the parsley pulp and $\frac{1}{4}$ cup of the basil pulp. Combine the parsley and basil juices, and set aside 1 tablespoon.

2. In a blender or food processor, combine the parsley pulp, basil pulp, and mixed juices with the remaining ingredients, and blend for 2 minutes, or until smooth.

3. Serve at room temperature over vegetables or whole grain pasta.

Makes 1 cup.

CHERRY YOGURT SAUCE

1 cup pitted cherries
(½ cup juice and ½ cup pulp)
1 cup plain yogurt

1. Juice the cherries. Set aside ½ cup of the juice and ½ cup of the pulp.

2. In a small mixing bowl, combine the juice, pulp, and yogurt, and stir until the mixture is well blended.

3. Serve cold with sliced fresh fruit, or spoon over cake.

Variations: Substitute strawberries, blueberries, or raspberries for the cherries.

Makes 2 cups.

GUACAMOLE
WITH BERMUDA ONION

2 lemons (3 tablespoons juice)

4 sprigs fresh cilantro (1 tablespoon pulp)

1 cup mashed avocado

¼ cup silken tofu

¼ teaspoon finely chopped jalapeño peppers

¼ teaspoon sea salt

¼ cup finely chopped red Bermuda onions

¼ cup finely chopped tomatoes

1. Separately juice the lemons and cilantro. Set aside 3 tablespoons of the lemon juice and 1 tablespoon of the cilantro pulp.

2. In a blender or food processor, combine the lemon juice, cilantro pulp, avocado, tofu, jalapeño peppers, and salt, and blend for 2 minutes, or until smooth.

3. Transfer the mixture to a small mixing bowl, add the remaining ingredients, and mix well with a spoon.

4. Serve cold or at room temperature with raw vegetables or corn chips.

Makes 1¾ cups.

TANGY
CARROT DIP

½ carrot (2 tablespoons juice)
¾ cup soft tofu
*½ cup cubed or mashed
steamed sweet potatoes*
2 tablespoons apple cider vinegar
¼ teaspoon ground cinnamon

1. Juice the carrot. Set aside 2 tablespoons of the juice.

2. In a blender or food processor, combine the carrot juice with the remaining ingredients, and blend for 2 minutes, or until smooth.

3. Serve cold with raw vegetables.

Makes 1½ cups.

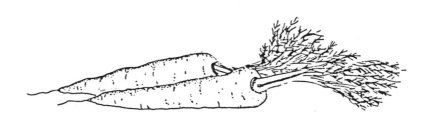

LEMONY HUMMUS

5 lemons (½ cup plus 2 tablespoons juice)
1 clove garlic (½ teaspoon pulp)
1½ cups sesame tahini
1 cup cooked garbanzo beans (chickpeas)
¼ cup water
½ teaspoon sea salt

1. Separately juice the lemons and garlic. Set aside ½ cup plus 2 tablespoons of the lemon juice, and ½ teaspoon of the garlic pulp.

2. In a blender or food processor, combine the lemon juice and garlic pulp with the remaining ingredients, and blend for 2 minutes, or until smooth.

3. Serve cold or at room temperature with raw vegetables or on bread.

Makes 3 cups.

BASIC MAYONNAISE

1 lemon (1½ tablespoons juice)
2 tablespoons apple cider vinegar
1 egg
¼ teaspoon sea salt
1¼ cups safflower oil

1. Juice the lemon. Set aside 1½ tablespoons of the juice.

2. In a blender or food processor, combine the lemon juice with the remaining ingredients, and blend for 2–3 minutes, or until smooth and creamy. Keep refrigerated in a covered glass jar.

3. Use as a spread for bread or in other recipes.

Makes 1½ cups.

BASIL MAYONNAISE

1 large bunch fresh basil (½ cup pulp)
2 cloves garlic (1 teaspoon pulp)
1 recipe Basic Mayonnaise (see above)

1. Separately juice the basil and garlic. Set aside ½ cup of the basil pulp and 1 teaspoon of the garlic pulp.
2. In a blender or food processor, combine the basil and garlic pulp with the Basic Mayonnaise, and blend for 2 minutes, or until smooth. Keep refrigerated in a covered glass jar.
3. Serve with raw vegetables.

Makes 2 cups.

DILL MAYONNAISE

1 large bunch fresh dill (½ cup pulp)
½ lemon (2 teaspoons juice)
1 recipe Basic Mayonnaise (see page 106)

1. Juice the dill and the lemon. Set aside ½ cup of the dill pulp and 2 teaspoons of the lemon juice.
2. In a blender or food processor, combine the dill pulp and lemon juice with the Basic Mayonnaise, and blend for 2 minutes, or until smooth. Keep refrigerated in a covered glass jar.
3. Serve with raw vegetables.

Makes 2 cups.

CURRY MAYONNAISE

$^3/_4$ *teaspoon ground cumin*

$^3/_4$ *teaspoon ground turmeric*

$^1/_4$ *teaspoon mustard powder*

$^1/_4$ *teaspoon ground ginger*

$^1/_8$ *teaspoon ground cinnamon*

$^1/_8$ *teaspoon cayenne pepper*

1 recipe Basic Mayonnaise (see page 106)

1. In a blender or food processor, combine all the ingredients, and blend for 2 minutes, or until smooth. Keep refrigerated in a covered glass jar.

2. Serve with raw vegetables.

Makes 1$^1/_2$ cups.

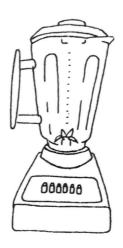

TOMATO SALSA

6 leaves fresh basil (1½ tablespoons pulp)
2 cups chopped tomatoes
¼ cup extra virgin olive oil
1 tablespoon crushed garlic
1 teaspoon sea salt
½ teaspoon black pepper

1. Juice the basil. Set aside 1½ tablespoons of the pulp.
2. In a small mixing bowl, combine the basil pulp with the remaining ingredients, and mix.
3. Serve cold or at room temperature with corn chips, on toast, or over whole grain pasta.

Makes 2¼ cups.

ORANGE
APRICOT SPREAD

12 oranges (3 cups juice and $\frac{1}{4}$ cup pulp)
$\frac{1}{2}$ cup chopped dried apricots
$\frac{1}{4}$ cup finely chopped orange peel
$\frac{1}{4}$ cup pure date sugar
2 tablespoons apple cider vinegar
1 tablespoon finely chopped red onion
dash of ground allspice

1. Juice the oranges. Set aside 3 cups juice and $\frac{1}{4}$ cup pulp.

2. In a medium-sized saucepan, bring the orange juice to a boil over high heat.

3. Reduce the heat to medium-low, add the remaining ingredients, and simmer for 15–20 minutes, or until the mixture reaches the consistency of spreadable preserves. Remove from the heat, and let cool before using.

4. Serve cold or at room temperature with breads and muffins.

Makes 2 cups.

CRANBERRY CHUTNEY

12 apples (3 cups juice and ½ cup pulp)
1 cup cranberries
½ cup chopped dried apricots
4 tablespoons pure date sugar
2 tablespoons apple cider vinegar
2 tablespoons diced red onions
¼ teaspoon ground allspice

1. Juice the apples. Set aside 3 cups of the juice and ½ cup of the pulp.

2. In a small saucepan, bring the apple juice to a boil over high heat.

3. Reduce the heat to medium-low, add the remaining ingredients, and simmer for 15–20 minutes, or until the mixture reaches the consistency of spreadable preserves. Remove from the heat, and let cool before using.

4. Serve cold or at room temperature with any vegetable dish.

Makes 2 cups.

STRAWBERRY BUTTER

1 pint strawberries ($\frac{1}{2}$ cup pulp)

*4 tablespoons ($\frac{1}{2}$ stick) softened sweet butter
or safflower oil-based margarine*

1. Juice the strawberries. Set aside $\frac{1}{2}$ cup of the pulp.

2. In a small mixing bowl, combine the strawberry pulp with the butter or margarine, and mix well with a whisk.

3. Serve at room temperature with breads and muffins.

Makes $\frac{3}{4}$ cup.

PEANUT BUTTER HONEY SPREAD

$\frac{1}{2}$ banana, frozen without peel ($\frac{1}{4}$ cup pulp)

1 cup unsalted peanuts

*3 tablespoons light-colored honey
(clover, tupelo, or wildflower)*

1. Juice the frozen banana. Set aside $\frac{1}{4}$ cup of the pulp (mashed banana).

2. In a blender, food processor, or food mill, blend the peanuts until they are smooth and creamy.

3. In a small mixing bowl, combine the banana pulp, peanut butter, and honey until well mixed.

4. Serve at room temperature with breads and muffins or fresh fruit slices.

Makes 1¼ cups.

BASIL HERB BUTTER

4 leaves fresh basil (1 tablespoon pulp)

2 cloves garlic (1 teaspoon pulp)

8 tablespoons (1 stick) softened sweet butter or safflower oil-based margarine

1 tablespoon extra virgin olive oil

¼ teaspoon sea salt

1. Separately juice the basil and garlic. Set aside 1 tablespoon of the basil pulp and 1 teaspoon of the garlic pulp.

2. In a small mixing bowl, combine the basil and garlic pulp with the remaining ingredients, and blend with a whisk until smooth.

3. Serve at room temperature with breads and muffins, or toss with hot whole grain pasta.

Makes ½ cup.

Main Dishes

FETTUCINE WITH PESTO AND TOMATOES

1 cup sliced mushrooms

1 cup broccoli florets

3 tablespoons extra virgin olive oil

3 cups cooked whole grain fettucine

1 recipe Walnut Pesto Sauce (see page 101)

1 cup chopped tomatoes

¼ cup grated Parmesan cheese, as garnish

1. In a large saucepan, sauté the mushrooms and broccoli in the oil over high heat for 3–5 minutes.

2. Reduce the heat to low, add the fettucine and Walnut Pesto Sauce, and toss.

3. Add the tomatoes, and toss.

4. Serve hot, garnished with the cheese.

Serves 2.

HALIBUT WITH TOMATO SALSA

2 eight-ounce halibut steaks

1 recipe Tomato Salsa (see page 109)

1. Preheat the broiler to 550°F.

2. Broil the halibut for 10 minutes, baste with the Tomato Salsa, turn the steaks over, baste again, and broil for an additional 5–7 minutes.

3. Serve with brown rice.

Serves 2.

STIR-FRIED BROCCOLI WITH TEMPEH AND LEMON THREADS

5 cups fresh basil (1 cup pulp)

1 small bunch fresh cilantro (¼ cup pulp)

2 lemons (¼ cup juice)

2 cloves garlic (1 teaspoon pulp)

1 lemon

¼ cup tamari soy sauce

1–2 tablespoons whole wheat flour

1 tablespoon apple cider vinegar

1 teaspoon chopped red chili peppers

1 teaspoon grated ginger root

2 cups tempeh, cut into 1-inch cubes

¼ cup toasted (dark) sesame oil

2½ cups broccoli florets

¼ cup sliced scallions

1 pint cherry tomatoes

1. Separately juice the basil, cilantro, 2 lemons, and garlic. Set aside 1 cup of the basil pulp, ¼ cup of the cilantro pulp, ¼ cup of the lemon juice, and 1 teaspoon of the garlic pulp.

2. Peel the remaining lemon, and slice the peel into threads. Set aside 1 tablespoon of the threads.

3. In a blender or food processor, combine the basil, cilantro, and garlic pulp with the lemon juice, soy sauce, flour, vinegar, peppers, and ginger, and blend for 2 minutes.

4. Transfer the basil mixture to a small saucepan, stir in the lemon peel threads, and heat for 4–5 minutes, or until warm.

5. In a large frying pan, brown the tempeh in the oil over medium to high heat.

6. Reduce the heat to medium-low, add the broccoli and scallions, cover, and cook for 2 minutes.

7. Add the tomatoes, and cook uncovered for 1 additional minute.

8. Arrange the tempeh mixture on a serving platter, and pour the heated sauce over the mixture.

9. Serve hot with brown rice.

Serves 2–3.

SCALLOPED
AUTUMN VEGETABLES

10 parsnips
($\frac{1}{2}$ cup juice and 2 tablespoons pulp)
$1\frac{1}{2}$ cups unsweetened soymilk
2 tablespoons chopped fresh parsley
1 tablespoon cold-pressed flavorless oil
(sunflower, safflower, or canola)
$\frac{1}{2}$ teaspoon sea salt
1 teaspoon chopped fresh thyme
or $\frac{1}{2}$ teaspoon dried thyme
$\frac{1}{2}$ teaspoon chopped fresh rosemary
or $\frac{1}{4}$ teaspoon dried rosemary
1 clove garlic, crushed
$1\frac{1}{2}$ cups sliced parsnips
1 cup sliced white potatoes
1 cup sliced acorn squash
$\frac{1}{2}$ cup chopped leeks
2 cups grated Swiss cheese, optional

1. Preheat the oven to 425°F.

2. Juice the parsnips. Set aside ½ cup of the juice
   and 2 tablespoons of the pulp.

3. In a small mixing bowl, combine the parsnip juice
   and pulp, soymilk, parsley, oil, salt, thyme, rosemary, and garlic, and mix well.

4. In a medium-sized mixing bowl, toss together the sliced parsnips, potatoes, squash, and leeks.

5. Arrange the vegetables on the bottom of a greased 9-by-12-inch baking dish or other large glass or ceramic dish. Pour the sauce over the vegetables, and sprinkle on the cheese, if desired. Cover with a glass lid or aluminum foil, and bake for 25 minutes, or until the vegetables are tender.

6. Serve hot with a salad or whole grain pasta.

Serves 4.

ZESTY CAULIFLOWER WITH GARLIC AND TAHINI

*1 recipe Tahini Garbanzo Bean Dressing
(see page 97)*

1 cup cauliflower florets

1 cup broccoli florets

1 cup sliced red bell peppers

½ cup unsalted whole cashews

½ cup diced red bell pepper, as garnish

4 sprigs fresh parsley, as garnish

1. Preheat the oven to 425°F.

2. In a medium-sized mixing bowl, combine the Tahini Garbanzo Bean Dressing, cauliflower, broccoli, sliced red pepper, and cashews, and toss to mix.

3. Pour the mixture into a greased 9-by-12-inch baking dish or other large glass or ceramic dish. Cover with a glass lid or aluminum foil, and bake for 25–35 minutes, or until the cauliflower is tender. (The other vegetables should still be crunchy.)

4. Garnish with the diced red pepper and parsley, and serve hot or cold with any rice or pasta dish.

Serves 2.

MATAR PANEER

1 tomato (½ cup juice)

16 ounces extra-firm tofu, cut into 1-inch cubes

2 tablespoons canola oil

¾ cup chopped yellow onions

2 cups frozen peas

1 cup chopped tomatoes

¾ cup unsweetened soymilk

3 teaspoons apple cider vinegar

½ cup finely chopped fresh cilantro

2 fresh green chili peppers, finely chopped

3 cloves garlic, crushed

2 teaspoons grated ginger root

1 teaspoon ground coriander

1 teaspoon ground turmeric

¼ teaspoon chili powder

1½ teaspoons sea salt

1. Juice the tomato. Set aside ½ cup of the juice.

2. In a large frying pan, brown the tofu in the oil over high heat.

3. Add the onions, and sauté for 2–3 minutes, or until the onions are soft.

4. Reduce the heat to medium-low, add the remaining ingredients, and simmer uncovered for an additional 5 minutes.

5. Serve hot with Peas Pillau With Cinnamon (see page 131).

Serves 4.

SALMON WITH TERIYAKI SAUCE

1 small piece ginger root
(1 teaspoon pulp)
¼ cup tamari soy sauce
1 clove garlic, crushed
1 tablespoon pure maple syrup
1 teaspoon sweet rice vinegar
2 eight-ounce salmon steaks

1. Preheat the broiler to 550°F.

2. Juice the ginger. Set aside 1 teaspoon of the pulp.

3. In a small mixing bowl, combine the ginger pulp, soy sauce, garlic, maple syrup, and vinegar, and mix well. Set aside.

4. Broil the salmon for 10 minutes, baste with the teriyaki sauce, turn the steaks over, baste again, and broil for an additional 5 minutes.

5. Serve with brown rice.

Serves 2.

MUSHROOMS STUFFED WITH HOLIDAY HERBS

2 cups mushrooms (½ cup pulp)
½ cup whole wheat bread crumbs
1 egg, beaten
1–3 tablespoons extra virgin olive oil
1½ tablespoons chopped fresh parsley
¼ teaspoon dried sage
¼ teaspoon dried rosemary
¼ teaspoon dried thyme
12 mushroom caps

1. Preheat the oven to 425°F.

2. Juice the 2 cups of mushrooms. Set aside ½ cup of the pulp.

3. In a small mixing bowl, combine the mushroom pulp with the bread crumbs, egg, oil, parsley, sage, rosemary, and thyme. Stuff the mushroom caps with the mixture.

4. Place the stuffed mushroom caps in an ungreased 9-by-12-inch baking dish, cover the dish with aluminum foil, and bake for 15–20 minutes.

5. Serve hot with a salad.

Serves 1.

MUSHROOM LASAGNA

4 carrots (1 cup pulp)

4 cups ricotta cheese

2 eggs, beaten

$\frac{1}{2}$ cup grated Parmesan cheese

$\frac{1}{4}$ cup chopped fresh parsley

$\frac{1}{2}$ teaspoon sea salt

$\frac{1}{4}$ teaspoon black pepper

2 cups broccoli florets

2 cups sliced mushrooms

3 tablespoons extra virgin olive oil

2 cups Zesty Tomato Sauce (see page 98)

1 pound cooked whole grain lasagna noodles

$3\frac{1}{2}$ cups shredded mozzarella cheese

1. Preheat the oven to 425°F.

2. Juice the carrots. Set aside 1 cup of the pulp.

3. In a medium-sized mixing bowl, combine the carrot pulp, ricotta cheese, eggs, Parmesan cheese, parsley, salt, and pepper, and mix well with a whisk. Set aside.

4. In a large saucepan, sauté the broccoli and mushrooms in the oil over high heat for 3–5 minutes. Set aside.

5. Spread 1 cup of the Zesty Tomato Sauce on the bottom of an ungreased 12-by-17-inch lasagna pan or baking dish. On top of the sauce, arrange a layer of lasagna noodles, a layer of broccoli and

mushrooms, a layer of the ricotta mixture, a layer of mozzarella cheese, and another layer of noodles. Repeat the layers, ending with additional layers of sauce and mozzarella.

6. Cover the lasagna with aluminum foil, and bake for 45–55 minutes. Let stand for 5 minutes before cutting.

7. Serve hot with a salad and whole grain bread.

Serves 6–8.

SWORDFISH WITH BASIL HERB BUTTER

2 eight-ounce swordfish steaks
1 recipe Basil Herb Butter (see page 113)

1. Preheat the broiler to 550°F.

2. Broil the swordfish for 10 minutes, baste with the Basil Herb Butter, turn the steaks over, baste again, and broil for an additional 10 minutes.

3. Serve with brown rice or whole grain pasta.

Serves 2.

MUSHROOM BROCCOLI QUICHE

1 tomato ($\frac{1}{2}$ cup juice)

1 large bunch fresh basil ($\frac{1}{2}$ cup pulp)

1 cup silken tofu

1 cup Guacamole With Bermuda Onion (see page 103)

$\frac{3}{4}$ cup grated Parmesan cheese

2 tablespoons extra virgin olive oil

$\frac{1}{8}$ teaspoon sea salt

$\frac{1}{8}$ teaspoon black pepper

$1\frac{1}{4}$ cups thinly sliced broccoli

$1\frac{1}{4}$ cups thinly sliced mushrooms

1 recipe Basic Wheat Crust, prebaked (see page 157)

1. Preheat the oven to 375°F.

2. Separately juice the tomato and basil. Set aside ½ cup of the tomato juice and ½ cup of the basil pulp.

3. In a blender or food processor, combine the tofu, Guacamole With Bermuda Onion, cheese, oil, salt, and pepper, and blend for 1 minute, or until creamy.

4. Arrange the broccoli and mushrooms on the bottom of the prepared Basic Wheat Crust. Pour the tofu mixture over the vegetables.

5. Bake the quiche uncovered for 25–30 minutes, or until the top of the quiche has set and begun to turn light brown in color. Remove the quiche from the oven, and let stand for 5 minutes before cutting.

6. Serve hot with a salad.

Serves 6–8.

SOLE WITH
WALNUT PESTO SAUCE

2 eight-ounce pieces of filet of sole

1 recipe Walnut Pesto Sauce (see page 101)

1. Preheat the broiler to 550°F.

2. Broil the sole for 10 minutes, baste with the Walnut Pesto Sauce, turn the filets over, baste again, and broil for an additional 5 minutes.

3. Serve with brown rice.

Serves 2.

ZESTY ITALIAN PIZZA

2 pieces whole wheat pita bread

1 cup chopped plum tomatoes with juice

1 packed cup chopped fresh basil

¼ cup chopped sun-dried tomatoes

*1 tablespoon Cilantro Pesto Sauce
(see page 99)*

½ teaspoon sea salt

¾ cup shredded mozzarella cheese

½ cup grated Parmesan cheese

1. Preheat the oven to 350°F.

2. In a small mixing bowl, combine the plum tomatoes, basil, sun-dried tomatoes, Cilantro Pesto Sauce, and salt, and mix well.

3. Place the pita bread on an ungreased cookie sheet, and spread with the tomato mixture. Sprinkle the top of each pizza with the mozzarella and Parmesan cheese.

4. Bake the pizzas for 15–20 minutes, or until the top is bubbly.

5. Serve hot with a salad.

Serves 2.

JAPANESE RICE WITH SHIITAKE MUSHROOMS

2-inch piece of ginger root
(2 tablespoons juice)
1½ cups sliced destemmed shiitake mushrooms
1 cup sliced zucchini
3 tablespoons safflower or other light oil
1 cup mung bean sprouts, drained
½ cup tamari soy sauce
3 teaspoons sliced scallions
4 cups cooked short-grain brown rice

1. Juice the ginger. Set aside 2 tablespoons of the juice.

2. In a large frying pan, sauté the mushrooms and zucchini in the oil over high heat until soft.

3. Reduce the heat to medium-low, add the ginger juice, bean sprouts, soy sauce, and scallions, and simmer for 1–2 minutes, or until the mixture has thickened.

4. Spoon the vegetable mixture over the rice, and serve hot.

Serves 2.

PEAS PILLAU WITH CINNAMON

4 carrots (1 cup juice)

2 teaspoons saffron threads

2 teaspoons water

1 cup uncooked white Basmati rice

3 tablespoons sesame oil

2 cups water

1½ cups frozen peas

1 tablespoon ground cardamom

1 stick cinnamon

1 teaspoon sea salt

½ teaspoon black pepper

1. Juice the carrots. Set aside 1 cup of the juice.

2. Dissolve the saffron threads in the 2 teaspoons of water.

3. In a medium-sized saucepan, sauté the rice in the oil over medium to high heat until the rice is light brown in color.

4. Add the carrot juice, saffron, and 2 cups of water, and bring the mixture to a boil over high heat. Reduce the heat to medium-low, cover, and cook for 12–15 minutes, or until all of the water is absorbed.

5. Stir in the remaining ingredients, and continue cooking until the mixture is hot.

6. Remove the cinnamon stick, and serve hot with Matar Paneer (see page 122) or a salad and whole grain bread.

Serves 2–4.

LENTIL BURGERS

4 carrots (½ cup pulp)

1 cup cooked red lentiis

¼ cup lentil sprouts

¼ cup ground unsalted cashews or
cashew butter

2 tablespoons chopped unsalted almonds

1 tablespoon diced yellow onions

2 teaspoons curry powder

½ teaspoon ground coriander

½ teaspoon sea salt

½ cup whole wheat bread crumbs

1. Preheat the oven to 425°F.

2. Juice the carrot. Set aside ½ cup of the pulp.

3. In a small mixing bowl, combine the carrot pulp
   with the lentils, lentil sprouts, cashews, almonds,
   onion, curry powder, coriander, and salt, and mix
   well.

4. Shape the mixture into 2 patties, coat the patties
   with the bread crumbs, and place them on an
   ungreased cookie sheet.

5. Bake the patties for 10 minutes, turn the patties
   over, and bake for an additional 10–15 minutes.

6. Serve hot in pita bread pockets with Lemony Hummus (see page 105).

Serves 2.

SPICY TEXAS CHILI

4 carrots (1 cup juice)
3 red or green bell peppers (¼ cup juice)
½ cup finely chopped yellow onions
¼ cup extra virgin olive oil
½ eggplant, chopped
½ cup cooked garbanzo beans (chickpeas)
½ cup cooked red kidney beans
½ cup sliced pattypan squash or zucchini
⅓ cup stewed tomatoes
¼ cup chopped green bell peppers
¼ cup corn kernels, fresh or frozen
¼ cup tomato purée
2½ teaspoons chopped green chili peppers
1 clove garlic, crushed

1. Separately juice the carrots and the 3 peppers. Set aside 1 cup of the carrot juice and ¼ cup of the pepper juice.

2. In a large saucepan, sauté the onions in the oil over high heat until the onions are soft.

3. Add the remaining ingredients to the saucepan, and bring to a boil. Reduce the heat to medium-low, and simmer uncovered for 15–20 minutes, or until the vegetables are tender.

4. Serve hot with corn bread or whole grain pasta.

Serves 2.

CURRIED
RED LENTIL STEW

2 carrots (½ cup juice)

2 stalks celery (½ cup juice)

1 beet (¼ cup juice)

¼ cup finely chopped yellow onions

2 tablespoons extra virgin olive oil

½ cup finely chopped tomatoes

3¾ cups water

¾ cup dried red lentils

1½ tablespoons finely chopped fresh cilantro

1 teaspoon dried parsley

1 teaspoon dried basil

¾ teaspoon curry powder

1 bay leaf

dash of ground cardamom

1¼ cups assorted frozen vegetables
(carrots, broccoli, and/or cauliflower)

1. Separately juice the carrots, celery, and beet. Set aside ½ cup of the carrot juice, ½ cup of the celery juice, and ¼ cup of the beet juice.

2. In a large saucepan, sauté the onions in the oil over high heat until the onions are soft.

3. Reduce the heat to medium-low, add the juices, tomatoes, water, and lentils, and cook uncovered for 15 minutes.

4. Add the cilantro, parsley, basil, curry powder, bay leaf, and cardamon, and cook for an additional 25 minutes.

5. Add the frozen vegetables, and cook, stirring occasionally, for another 15 minutes, or until the vegetables are tender and the lentils are done.

6. Serve hot with brown rice.

Serves 2.

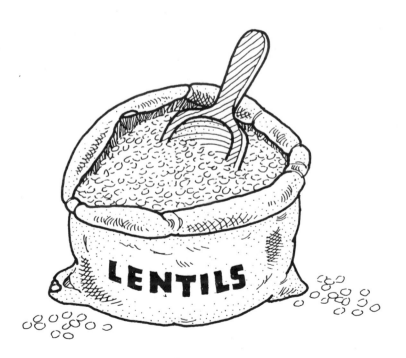

Desserts

CHERRY FRUIT POPS

1 lemon (2 tablespoons juice)
3 cups frozen pitted cherries
(or any other frozen berries)

1. Juice the lemons. Set aside 2 tablespoons of the juice.

2. In a blender or food processor, combine the lemon juice and cherries, and blend for 2 minutes, or until smooth.

3. Pour the mixture into six 5-ounce ice-pop molds, and freeze for 3–4 hours, or until firm.

Makes 6 pops.

APPLE PECAN COBBLER

Filling

2 pears ($\frac{1}{2}$ cup juice and $\frac{3}{4}$ cup pulp)
2 apples ($\frac{1}{2}$ cup juice and $\frac{3}{4}$ cup pulp)
1 orange ($\frac{1}{4}$ cup juice)
$\frac{1}{2}$ lemon (1 tablespoon juice)
$3\frac{1}{2}$ cups sliced apples, unpeeled
$\frac{1}{2}$ teaspoon ground cinnamon
$\frac{2}{3}$ cup chopped apricots (dried or fresh)

Topping

3 cups coarsely chopped unsalted pecans
1 cup coarsely chopped unsalted
macadamia nuts
1 cup pure maple syrup
5 tablespoons safflower margarine
or sweet butter
2 teaspoons pure almond extract
1 teaspoon grated orange peel
2 teaspoons ground cinnamon
$\frac{1}{4}$ cup pure date sugar

1. Preheat the oven to 400°F.

2. Separately juice the pears, the 2 apples (not the slices), the orange, and the lemon. Set aside $\frac{1}{2}$ cup

of the pear juice and ¾ cup of the pear pulp, ½ cup of the apple juice and ¾ cup of the apple pulp, ¼ cup of the orange juice, and 1 tablespoon of the lemon juice.

3. In a medium-sized mixing bowl, combine the apple slices with the pear, apple, and orange juices. Stir in the pear and apple pulp, lemon juice, cinnamon, and apricots, mixing well.

4. In another medium-sized mixing bowl, combine all the topping ingredients except the sugar and 1 teaspoon of the cinnamon, mixing well.

5. In a small mixing bowl, combine the sugar with the remaining 1 teaspoon of cinnamon, and mix well.

6. Pour the apple slice mixture into a greased 9-by-12-inch baking dish, spreading the filling evenly so that it touches all sides of the pan.

7. Pour the topping over the filling, and spread it evenly with a knife.

8. Bake the cobbler for 30–35 minutes, or until the apples are soft. Remove from the oven, and sprinkle with the sugar-cinnamon mixture.

9. Serve hot or cold with ice cream.

Serves 6–8.

CORN CRISPIES TREATS

1 parsnip (¼ cup pulp)
½ cup plus 2 tablespoons sweet rice syrup
¼ cup peanut butter
1½ teaspoons pure almond extract
3 cups unsweetened corn flakes
¼ cup chopped dates

1. Juice the parsnip. Set aside ¼ cup of the pulp.

2. In a 2-quart saucepan, combine the rice syrup, peanut butter, and almond extract, and bring to a simmer.

3. Remove the mixture from the heat, and stir in the parsnip pulp, corn flakes, and dates, mixing together well.

4. Spoon the mixture into a greased 9-by-12-inch baking dish, and press down firmly.

5. Cool completely before slicing into 9 bars.

Makes 9 bars.

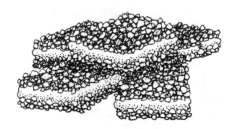

CARROT WALNUT CAKE

2 oranges (¹⁄₂ cup juice)

2 sweet potatoes, steamed and chilled (1 cup juice)

6 carrots (1¹⁄₂ cups pulp)

1¹⁄₂ cups unsalted walnut halves

³⁄₄ cup unsalted pecan halves

2 eggs

1 cup cold-pressed flavorless oil (sunflower, safflower, or canola)

1 cup light-colored honey (clover, tupelo, or wildflower)

2 teaspoons pure almond extract

4¹⁄₂ cups stone-ground whole wheat flour

2¹⁄₄ teaspoons baking powder

1¹⁄₄ teaspoons baking soda

1 teaspoon ground cinnamon

¹⁄₂ teaspoon ground nutmeg

¹⁄₄ teaspoon ground cloves

1 cup chopped dates

1. Preheat the oven to 350°F.

2. Separately juice the oranges, sweet potatoes, and carrots. Set aside ¹⁄₂ cup of the orange juice, 1 cup of the sweet potato juice (carrot juice may be substituted), and 1¹⁄₂ cups of the carrot pulp.

3. In the oven, toast the walnuts and pecans on an ungreased cookie sheet for approximately 10 minutes, stirring occasionally. (Be careful not to let them burn, as this causes bitterness.) Coarsely chop the nuts and set aside.

4. In a medium-sized mixing bowl, combine the orange and sweet potato juices, eggs, oil, honey, and almond extract, and mix well. Stir in the carrot pulp.

5. In a large mixing bowl, sift the flour with the baking powder, baking soda, cinnamon, nutmeg, and cloves.

6. Add the egg mixture to the flour mixture, and blend with an electric hand-held mixer until smooth. Add the dates and toasted nuts to the batter, and mix well.

7. Pour the batter into 2 greased 3-by-7-inch loaf pans, and bake for 45 minutes to 1 hour, or until a toothpick inserted in the center of the loaves comes out clean.

8. Allow the loaves to cool for about 5 minutes before removing from the pans. Cool the loaves for at least 5 additional minutes before slicing.

Makes two 3-by-7-inch loaves.

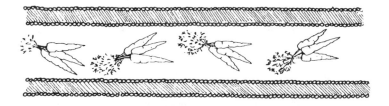

BANANA ALMOND BREAD

1 banana, frozen without peel ($\frac{1}{2}$ cup pulp)

1 egg

*$\frac{1}{2}$ cup light-colored honey
(clover, tupelo, or wildflower)*

*$\frac{1}{3}$ cup cold-pressed flavorless oil
(sunflower, safflower, or canola)*

1 teaspoon pure almond extract

1 $\frac{1}{4}$ cups plus 1 tablespoon whole wheat flour

1 teaspoon baking soda

$\frac{1}{2}$ teaspoon ground nutmeg

$\frac{1}{2}$ teaspoon ground cinnamon

$\frac{1}{4}$ teaspoon sea salt

$\frac{1}{2}$ cup water

$\frac{1}{4}$ cup slivered blanched almonds

1. Preheat the oven to 350°F.

2. Juice the frozen banana. Set aside $\frac{1}{2}$ cup of the pulp (mashed banana).

3. In a medium-sized mixing bowl, combine the egg, honey, oil, and almond extract.

4. In a small mixing bowl, sift together the flour, baking soda, nutmeg, cinnamon, and salt.

5. Add a small amount of the flour mixture to the egg mixture, and blend well. Then add a small amount

of the water to the egg mixture, and blend well. Alternate adding the remaining flour mixture and the water to the egg mixture, making sure to blend well after each addition.

6. Add the banana and almonds to the batter, and mix well with a sturdy spoon.

7. Pour the batter into a greased 3-by-7-inch loaf pan. Bake for 15 minutes, remove the loaf from the oven, and make a 1-inch-deep slice lengthwise down the center of the loaf (this facilitates cooking the center). Return the loaf to the oven, and bake for an additional 25–30 minutes, or until a toothpick inserted in the center comes out clean.

8. Allow the bread to cool for 5 minutes before removing it from the pan. Cool the bread for at least 5 additional minutes before slicing.

Makes one 3-by-7-inch loaf.

PUMPKIN AND SPICE MUFFINS

*1 sweet potato, steamed and chilled
(½ cup juice)*

½ small pumpkin (¾ cup pulp)

¾ cup unsalted walnut halves

2 eggs

*½ cup plus 2 tablespoons cold-pressed
flavorless oil (sunflower, safflower,
or canola)*

½ cup pure date sugar

1 banana, mashed

1 teaspoon pure vanilla extract

2 cups stone-ground whole wheat flour

1 teaspoon baking powder

1 teaspoon baking soda

1 teaspoon ground nutmeg

½ teaspoon ground allspice

½ teaspoon ground cinnamon

½ cup raisins

1. Preheat the oven to 350°F.

2. Separately juice the sweet potato and pumpkin.
   Set aside ½ cup of the sweet potato juice (pumpkin juice may be subsituted), and ¾ cup of the
   pumpkin pulp.

3. In the oven, toast the walnuts on an ungreased cookie sheet for approximately 10 minutes, stirring occasionally. (Be careful not to let them burn, as this causes bitterness.) Coarsely chop the nuts and set aside.

4. In a medium-sized mixing bowl, combine the sweet potato juice, eggs, oil, sugar, banana, and vanilla extract, and mix well with a sturdy spoon. Add the pumpkin pulp to the mixture, and stir.

5. In a small mixing bowl, sift together the flour, baking powder, baking soda, nutmeg, allspice, and cinnamon.

6. Add the flour mixture to the egg mixture, and blend well. Stir in the toasted nuts and raisins.

7. Pour the batter into greased or paper-lined muffin tins, and bake for 25–30 minutes, or until a toothpick inserted in the center of a muffin comes out clean.

Makes 24 muffins.

ALMOND
BUTTER COOKIES

2–3 parsnips ($\frac{1}{3}$ cup pulp)

$\frac{1}{4}$ cup almonds

8 tablespoons (1 stick) sweet butter, softened

*$\frac{1}{3}$ cup light-colored honey
(clover, tupelo, or wildflower)*

2 teaspoons pure almond extract

3 cups flour

2 tablespoons baking powder

1 teaspoon sea salt

$1\frac{1}{2}$ teaspoons ground cinnamon

*$\frac{1}{2}$ cup ground unsalted almonds or
almond butter*

$\frac{1}{4}$ cup pure date sugar

1. Juice the parsnips. Set aside $\frac{1}{3}$ cup of the pulp.

2. In the oven, toast the almonds on an ungreased cookie sheet for approximately 10 minutes, stirring occasionally. (Be careful not to let them burn, as this causes bitterness.) In a blender, food processor, or food mill, grind the nuts and set aside.

3. In a medium-sized mixing bowl, cream together the butter, honey, and almond extract.

4. In another medium-sized mixing bowl, sift together the flour, baking powder, salt, and 1 teaspoon of the cinnamon.

5. Add the flour mixture to the butter mixture, and stir to blend. Stir in the ½ cup ground almonds (or almond butter) and the parsnip pulp, blending thoroughly with a sturdy spoon.

6. Roll the dough into a log, and cover with plastic wrap. Chill for 1 hour.

7. Preheat the oven to 350°F.

8. In a small mixing bowl, combine the remaining ½ teaspoon of cinnamon with the sugar and the ground toasted almonds.

9. Remove the cookie dough from the refrigerator. On a floured surface, roll the dough to ¼-inch thickness with a rolling pin, and use cookie cutters to cut the dough into the desired shapes. Sprinkle the shapes with the cinnamon-sugar mixture, and bake on an ungreased cookie sheet for 10–15 minutes, or until the cookies are light brown along the edges.

Makes 18 cookies.

HOLIDAY
SURPRISE COOKIES

2 sweet potatoes, steamed and chilled
(1 cup pulp)

1 cup unsalted pecan halves

1 cup unsalted walnut halves

2 eggs

1½ cups pure date sugar

2 tablespoons pure maple syrup

1 cup (2 sticks) sweet butter, softened

1 teaspoon pure vanilla extract

1 teaspoon pure almond extract

1⅔ cups plus 2 tablespoons whole wheat flour

1 teaspoon baking soda

1 teaspoon baking powder

1 teaspoon ground cinnamon

½ teaspoon sea salt

1½ cups raisins

1 cup rolled oats

½ cup unsweetened carob chips

¼ cup unsweetened flaked coconut

¼ cup unsalted hulled sunflower seeds

1. Preheat the oven to 375°F.

2. Juice the sweet potatoes. Set aside 1 cup of the
   pulp.

3. In the oven, toast the pecans and walnuts on an ungreased cookie sheet for approximately 10 minutes, stirring occasionally. (Be careful not to let them burn, as this causes bitterness.) Coarsely chop the nuts and set aside.

4. In a medium-sized mixing bowl, combine the sweet potato pulp, eggs, sugar, maple syrup, butter, and vanilla and almond extracts. Blend well with an electric hand-held mixer.

5. In a small mixing bowl, sift together the flour, baking soda, baking powder, cinnamon, and salt.

6. Add the flour mixture to the sweet potato mixture, and blend well with a sturdy spoon. Stir in the toasted nuts, raisins, oats, carob chips, coconut, and sunflower seeds, and mix well.

7. Roll the dough into ¼-inch balls. Place the balls on an ungreased cookie sheet, and bake for 15 minutes, or until the cookies turn light brown in color.

Makes 30 cookies.

FRUIT AND NUT COOKIES

1 carrot (⅛ cup pulp)

½ cup unsalted pecan halves

¾ cup whole unsalted almonds

1 egg

4 tablespoons (½ stick) sweet butter, softened

1 cup pure date sugar

2 tablespoons pure maple syrup

¼ teaspoon pure vanilla extract

½ teaspoon pure almond extract

¾ cup whole wheat flour

½ teaspoon baking soda

⅛ teaspoon sea salt

½ cup unsweetened carob chips

¼ cup rolled oats

½ cup raisins

1. Preheat the oven to 375°F.

2. Juice the carrot. Set aside ⅛ cup of the pulp.

3. In the oven, toast the pecans and almonds on an ungreased cookie sheet for approximately 10 minutes, stirring occasionally. (Be careful not to let them burn, as this causes bitterness.) Coarsely chop the nuts and set aside.

4. In a medium-sized mixing bowl, cream together the egg, butter, sugar, maple syrup, and vanilla and almond extracts. Add the carrot pulp, and mix well.

5. In a small mixing bowl, sift together the flour, baking soda, and salt.

6. Add the flour mixture to the carrot mixture, and blend well with a sturdy spoon. Stir in the nuts, carob chips, oats, and raisins.

7. Roll the dough into ¼-inch balls. Place the balls on an ungreased cookie sheet, and bake for 15 minutes, or until the cookies are golden brown in color.

Makes 18 cookies.

DATE FUDGE BROWNIES

3 parsnips ($\frac{1}{2}$ cup pulp)
1 cup whole wheat flour
1 teaspoon baking powder
$\frac{1}{2}$ cup safflower oil
1 egg
$\frac{1}{4}$ cup pure maple syrup
1 cup pure unsweetened cocoa powder (unsweetened carob powder may be substituted)
$1\frac{1}{2}$ cups pure date sugar
1 teaspoon pure vanilla extract
$\frac{1}{2}$ cup ground unsalted almonds or almond butter
1 cup coarsely chopped unsalted walnuts
$\frac{3}{4}$ cup chopped dates

1. Preheat the oven to 350°F.

2. Juice the parsnips. Set aside ½ cup of the pulp.

3. In a small mixing bowl, sift together the flour and baking powder.

4. In a large mixing bowl, combine the oil, egg, maple syrup, and cocoa. Add the parsnip pulp, sugar, and vanilla extract, and mix well. Add the flour mixture, and mix again. Stir in the almonds, walnuts, and dates.

5. Pour the batter into a greased 10-inch square pan, and bake for 30–40 minutes, or until firm.

6. Allow to cool slightly before cutting into 12 squares.

Makes 12 brownies.

PECAN CHEWIES

6 parsnips (1 cup pulp)
1½ cups sweet rice syrup
½ cup raw almond butter
3 teaspoons pure almond extract
2 cups coarsely chopped unsalted pecans
1 cup blanched slivered almonds

1. Preheat the oven to 350°F.

2. Juice the parsnips. Set aside 1 cup of the pulp.

3. In a medium-sized mixing bowl, combine the sweet rice syrup, almond butter, and almond extract. Add the parsnip pulp, pecans, and almonds, and mix well.

4. Pour the mixture into a greased 9-inch square baking dish, and bake for 10 minutes, or until the nuts begin to turn light brown in color.

5. Cool for about 5 minutes before cutting into 6 squares.

Makes 6 chewies.

CAROB FRUIT BARS

4 carrots (1 cup pulp)

¾ cup pure maple syrup

2 eggs

*¼ cup light-colored honey
(clover, tupelo, or wildflower)*

1 teaspoon pure almond extract

½ teaspoon ground cinnamon

1 cup mashed banana

1 cup unsweetened flaked coconut

¾ cup unsweetened carob chips

1 cup coarsely chopped unsalted pecans

*¼ cup coarsely chopped unsalted macadamia
nuts (pecans may be substituted)*

4 tablespoons (½ stick) sweet butter, softened

½ cup whole wheat flour

1. Preheat the oven to 375°F.

2. Juice the carrots. Set aside 1 cup of the pulp.

3. In a medium-sized mixing bowl, whisk together the maple syrup, eggs, honey, almond extract, and cinnamon. Add the carrot pulp, banana, coconut, carob chips, pecans, and macadamia nuts, and stir well.

4. In another medium-sized mixing bowl, combine the butter and flour, and blend until a dough forms.

5. Press the dough into a greased 9-by-12-inch baking dish. Pour the maple syrup mixture over the crust, and bake for 15–20 minutes.

6. Allow to cool for 10 minutes before slicing into 12 bars.

Makes 12 bars.

DATE NUT CRUST

3 parsnips (½ cup pulp)

3 cups whole pitted dates

1½ cups unsalted pecans, soaked and drained

1. Juice the parsnips. Set aside ½ cup of the pulp.

2. In a blender or food processor, combine the parsnip pulp, dates, and pecans, and blend until smooth.

3. Press the mixture into a lightly greased 9-inch pie plate (or a 9-by-12-inch baking dish).

4. When a recipe calls for a baked crust, put the crust in a 350°F oven for 15 minutes, or until light brown in color.

Makes one 9-inch crust.

BASIC
WHEAT CRUST

½ cup whole wheat flour

½ cup unbleached white flour

½ teaspoon ground cinnamon

⅓ cup cold sweet butter

¼ cup plus 3 tablespoons cold water, buttermilk, or unsweetened soymilk

1. In a small mixing bowl, combine the whole wheat flour, white flour, and cinnamon.

2. With a fork or pastry cutter, cut the butter into the flour mixture until the mixture is moist and fine. Add the cold water (or milk) by the tablespoon until the dough has a smooth, even consistency.

3. Roll the dough into a ball, and place it in a bowl. Cover the bowl with plastic wrap, and chill for 1 hour.

4. Flour a smooth, clean surface and a rolling pin with all-purpose flour. Place the chilled dough on the floured surface, and roll the dough from the center out until it is ½ inch larger than a 9-inch pie plate. (Check by placing the empty pie plate on top of the rolled dough.)

5. Loosen the dough by gently sliding a floured spatula underneath it toward the center, and moving around the entire area of the dough until it can be lifted. Transfer the dough to a lightly greased 9-inch pie plate.

6. When a recipe calls for a baked crust, put the crust in a 350°F oven for 15 minutes, or until light brown in color.

Makes one 9-inch crust.

SWEET POTATO CRUST

*4 sweet potatoes, steamed and chilled
(2 cups pulp)*

1 egg

¼ cup finely chopped dates

½ teaspoon pure almond extract

1. Preheat the oven to 350°F.

2. Juice the sweet potatoes. Set aside 2 cups of the pulp.

3. In a small mixing bowl, combine the sweet potato pulp, egg, dates, and almond extract, and mix together well.

4. Press the mixture into a lightly greased 9-inch pie plate (or a 9-by-12-inch baking dish), and bake for 40 minutes, or until golden brown in color.

Makes one 9-inch crust.

SWEET POTATO PIE

1 apple (¹/₄ cup juice)
3 cups mashed steamed sweet potatoes
2 eggs
¹/₄ cup pure maple syrup
1¹/₂ teaspoons ground allspice
1 recipe Basic Wheat Crust, prebaked
(see page 157)

1. Preheat the oven to 350°F.

2. Juice the apple. Set aside ¼ cup of the juice.

3. In a blender or food processor, combine the apple juice, sweet potatoes, eggs, maple syrup, and allspice, and blend until smooth.

4. Pour the sweet potato mixture into the prepared pie crust, and bake for 25 minutes, or until the crust is golden and the filling is set.

5. Allow the pie to cool for 10 minutes before serving.

Makes one 9-inch pie.

TROPICAL AMBROSIA PUDDING

1 tangerine (¼ cup juice)

1 mango (½ cup juice)

¼ pineapple (¼ cup juice)

1½ cups silken tofu

¼ cup pure maple syrup

2 teaspoons pure almond extract

¼ teaspoon ground nutmeg

¾ cup mashed banana

3 tablespoons unsweetened flaked coconut

3 tablespoons raisins

3 tablespoons blanched slivered almonds

1. Separately juice the tangerine, mango, and pineapple. Set aside ¼ cup of the tangerine juice, ½ cup of the mango juice, and ¼ cup of the pineapple juice.

2. In a blender or food processor, combine the juices with the silken tofu, and blend for 2–3 minutes, or until smooth.

3. Add the maple syrup, almond extract, and nutmeg, and continue to blend.

4. Transfer the mixture to a small mixing bowl, and stir in the banana, coconut, raisins, and almonds.

5. Chill for at least 1 hour before serving.

Serves 2 to 4.

APPLESAUCE

5 apples (1¼ cups juice and 1 cup pulp)
1 tablespoon raisins
dash of ground cinnamon

1. Juice the apples. Set aside 1¼ cups of the juice and 1 cup of the pulp.

2. In a small saucepan, bring the apple juice to a boil over high heat.

3. Reduce the heat to medium-low, and add the apple pulp, raisins, and cinnamon. Simmer for 5–10 minutes.

4. Serve hot or cold.

Makes 1½ cups.

STRAWBERRY COMPOTE WITH SAFFRON FLOWERS

¼ pineapple (¼ cup juice)
1 teaspoon saffron threads
1 cup sliced strawberries
1 cup mashed banana
¼ teaspoon ground nutmeg

1. Juice the pineapple. Set aside ¼ cup of the juice.

2. In a small saucepan, combine the pineapple juice with the saffron threads. Cook over medium heat until the mixture comes to a simmer, and remove from the heat.

3. In a blender or food processor, combine the pineapple mixture with the remaining ingredients, and blend for two minutes, or until smooth. Transfer to a small bowl, and chill for 1 hour.

4. Serve cold over cake or ice cream.

Makes 2 cups.

BANANA
COCOA SUNDAE

2 bananas, frozen without peel
(1 cup pulp)

2 tablespoons pure unsweetened cocoa powder
(unsweetened carob powder may be
substituted)

2 tablespoons unsweetened flaked coconut

1. Juice the frozen bananas, and collect 1 cup of the pulp (mashed banana) in a small mixing bowl.

2. Add the cocoa to the pulp, and mix together well.

3. Divide the mixture into two serving dishes, top with the coconut, and serve cold.

Makes 2 sundaes.

BANANA NUTMEG SUNDAE WITH PINEAPPLE AND COCONUT

2 bananas, frozen without peel (1 cup pulp)
¼ cup fresh pineapple chunks
2 tablespoons unsweetened flaked coconut
¼ teaspoon ground nutmeg

1. Juice the frozen bananas, and collect 1 cup of the pulp (mashed banana).

2. Divide the banana pulp into two serving dishes, top with the remaining ingredients, and serve cold.

Makes 2 sundaes.

STRAWBERRY CHOCOLATE POPS

2 bananas, frozen without peel (1 cup pulp)

4 cups peeled honeydew melon chunks
(1⅓ cups juice)

1 cup frozen strawberries

1 tablespoon pure unsweetened cocoa powder
(unsweetened carob powder may be
substituted)

1 teaspoon pure lemon extract

1. Separately juice the frozen bananas and the melon. Set aside 1 cup of the banana pulp (mashed banana) and 1⅓ cups of the melon juice.

2. In a blender or food processor, combine the banana pulp and melon juice with the remaining ingredients, and blend for 2 minutes, or until smooth.

3. Pour the mixture into six 5-ounce ice-pop molds, and freeze for 3–4 hours, or until firm.

Makes 6 pops.

CREAMSICLE POPS

8 oranges (2 cups juice)

1 cup plain yogurt

¼ cup unsweetened flaked coconut

*¼ cup ground unsalted almonds
or almond butter*

1 tablespoon pure vanilla extract

1. Juice the oranges. Set aside 2 cups of the juice.

2. In a blender or food processor, combine the juice with the remaining ingredients, and blend for 2 minutes, or until smooth.

3. Pour the mixture into six 5-ounce ice-pop molds, and freeze for 3–4 hours, or until firm.

Makes 6 pops

CHOCOLATE COCONUT POPS

2 bananas, frozen without peel (1 cup pulp)

6 oranges (1½ cups juice)

½ cup plain yogurt

¼ cup unsweetened flaked coconut

2 tablespoons pure unsweetened cocoa powder (unsweetened carob powder may be substituted)

2 tablespoons ground unsalted pecans or pecan butter

2 teaspoons pure almond extract

1. Separately juice the frozen bananas and the oranges. Set aside 1 cup of the banana pulp (mashed banana) and 1½ cups of the orange juice.

2. In a blender or food processor, combine the banana pulp and orange juice with the remaining ingredients, and blend for two minutes, or until smooth.

3. Pour the mixture into six 5-ounce ice-pop molds, and freeze for 3–4 hours, or until firm.

Makes 6 pops.

RASPBERRY MELON POPS

4 cups peeled watermelon chunks
(1⅓ cups juice)

2 cups peeled honeydew melon chunks
(⅔ cup juice)

2 lemons (¼ cup juice)

1½ cups frozen raspberries

2 teaspoons lemon extract

1. Separately juice the watermelon, honeydew melon, and lemons. Set aside 1⅓ cups of the watermelon juice, ⅔ cup of the honeydew melon juice, and ¼ cup of the lemon juice.

2. In a blender or food processor, combine the juices with the remaining ingredients, and blend for 2 minutes, or until smooth.

3. Pour the mixture into six 5-ounce ice-pop molds, and freeze for 3–4 hours, or until firm.

Makes 6 pops.

KIWI LIME POPS

6 kiwis (1½ cups juice)

*4 cups peeled honeydew melon chunks
(1⅓ cups juice)*

2 lemons (3 tablespoons juice)

2 limes (3 tablespoons juice)

1. Separately juice the kiwis, melon, lemons, and limes. Set aside 1½ cups of the kiwi juice, 1⅓ cups of the melon juice, 3 tablespoons of the lemon juice, and 3 tablespoons of the lime juice.

2. In a small mixing bowl, combine the juices, mixing well with a spoon.

3. Pour the mixture into six 5-ounce ice-pop molds, and freeze for 3–4 hours, or until firm.

Makes 6 pops.

TROPICAL POPS

6 apples (1½ cups juice)

3 carrots (⅔ cup juice)

2 bananas, frozen without peel (1 cup pulp)

3 tablespoons chopped dates

3 tablespoons unsweetened flaked coconut

3 tablespoons ground unsalted almonds
or almond butter

1 teaspoon ground nutmeg

1 teaspoon pure almond extract

1. Separately juice the apples, carrots, and frozen bananas. Set aside 1½ cups of the apple juice, ⅔ cup of the carrot juice, and 1 cup of the banana pulp (mashed banana).

2. In a blender or food processor, combine the juices and pulp with the remaining ingredients, and blend for 2 minutes, or until smooth.

3. Pour the mixture into six 5-ounce ice-pop molds, and freeze for 3–4 hours, or until firm.

Makes 6 pops.

GINGERBREAD

1 small piece ginger root
(¼ teaspoon juice and ¼ teaspoon pulp)
⅓ cup safflower oil
½ cup light-colored honey
(tupelo, clover, or wildflower)
⅓ cup unsulphured blackstrap molasses
1 egg
¼ cup pure date sugar
½ cup unsweetened soymilk
¼ cup water
1¾ cups plus 1 tablespoon whole wheat flour
1 teaspoon baking powder
½ teaspoon ground cinnamon
¼ teaspoon ground nutmeg
¼ teaspoon sea salt
1 recipe Cocoa Coconut Frosting (see page 172)

1. Preheat the oven to 350°F.

2. Juice the ginger. Set aside ¼ teaspoon of the juice and ¼ teaspoon of the pulp.

3. In a medium-sized mixing bowl, combine the ginger juice and pulp, oil, honey, molasses, egg, sugar, soymilk, and water. Stir the ingredients well.

4. In a small mixing bowl, sift together the flour, baking powder, cinnamon, nutmeg, and salt. Add to the oil mixture, and blend well.

5. Grease the bottom of a 9-inch round or 10-inch square baking pan, line with parchment paper, and regrease. Pour the batter into the pan, and bake for 15–20 minutes, or until a toothpick inserted in the center of the cake comes out clean.

6. Allow the cake to cool for 5 minutes before removing it from the pan. Remove the parchment paper, and cool completely before glazing with Cocoa Coconut Frosting.

Makes one 9-inch cake.

Cocoa Coconut Frosting

*¾ cup light-colored honey
(clover, tupelo, or wildflower)*

*¼ cup plus 2 tablespoons pure unsweetened
cocoa powder (unsweetened carob powder
may be substituted)*

3 tablespoons plain yogurt (optional)

1 teaspoon pure almond extract

2 tablespoons unsweetened flaked coconut

1. In a small mixing bowl, whisk together all of the ingredients, except the coconut, until a smooth frosting is formed.

2. Add the coconut, and mix well.

Makes 1 cup.

MANGO FRUIT POPS

4 mangos (2 cups juice)
1½ pineappples (1½ cups juice)
1½ lemons (3 tablespoons juice)

1. Separately juice the mangos, pineapples, and lemons. Set aside 2 cups of the mango juice, 1½ cups of the pineapple juice, and 3 tablespoons of the lemon juice.

2. In a small mixing bowl, combine the juices, mixing well with a spoon.

3. Pour the mixture into six 5-ounce ice-pop molds, and freeze for 3–4 hours, or until firm.

Makes 6 pops.

The Seven-Day Menu Plan

The following menu plan shows how you can use the recipes presented in *The Joy of Juicing* to eat a balanced, varied diet that incorporates the high-nutrient content of fruit and vegetable juices into every meal. Each day, the plan provides a wide range of vitamins, minerals, complex carbohydrates, and proteins, as well as a variety of tastes and textures. Naturally, this menu plan is meant only to provide guidelines and stir your culinary imagination. Feel free to substitute some of your own favorite recipes for those listed below—being sure to emphasize fresh fruits, vegetables, and grains, and healthful juices. Be aware that this plan is not meant as a weight-loss diet, but is instead a health-maintenance diet. However, by limiting portion size and modifying the menu, as well as your lifestyle, according to Gary Null's Natural-Living Weight-Loss Tips (see page 179), you will have a personalized plan that will help you lose weight *without* sacrificing good nutrition.

DAY ONE

Breakfast Juice:	Refreshing Watercress Juice 1 scoop protein powder (optional, see pages 4–5)
Breakfast:	Sweet Rice Cream Cereal
Snack:	Holiday Surprise Cookies
Lunch:	Mushroom Barley Soup and Tabouli Salad
Snack:	Lemony Hummus with rice cakes or pita bread
Dinner Juice:	Tangy Purple Cabbage Surprise
Dinner:	Scalloped Autumn Vegetables

DAY TWO

Breakfast Juice:	Lemon Cucumber Juice 1 scoop protein powder (optional)
Breakfast:	Tropical Millet Delight
Snack:	1 slice Banana Almond Bread
Lunch:	Creamy Tomato Soup and Zesty Tuna Salad
Snack:	Applesauce
Dinner Juice:	Swiss Chard Celery Juice
Dinner:	Salmon with Teriyaki Sauce and Japanese Rice with Shiitake Mushrooms

DAY THREE

Breakfast Juice:	Grandma's Mixed Vegetable Juice 1 scoop protein powder (optional)
Breakfast:	Barley Cereal with Apples and Spice

Snack:	1 Carob Fruit Bar
Lunch:	Mixed Dark Green Salad and Celery Potato Soup
Snack:	Mushrooms Stuffed with Holiday Herbs
Dinner Juice:	Cranberry Pineapple Cocktail
Dinner:	Spicy Texas Chili

DAY FOUR

Breakfast Juice:	Honeydew Melon Shake 1 scoop protein powder (optional)
Breakfast:	Hearty Oats with Nuts and Raisins
Snack:	1 wedge Sweet Potato Pie
Lunch:	Southwestern Squash Soup and Tomato Garlic Pasta Salad
Snack:	Guacamole with Bermuda Onion
Dinner Juice:	Lemon Kiwi Spritzer
Dinner:	Sole with Walnut Pesto Sauce

DAY FIVE

Breakfast Juice:	Cauliflower Beet Juice 1 scoop protein powder (optional)
Breakfast:	Western Omelet
Snack:	1 slice Carrot Walnut Cake
Lunch:	Vegetable Millet Soup and Mixed Sprout Salad
Snack:	Peanut Butter Honey Spread with celery sticks

Dinner Juice:	Citrus Tonic
Dinner:	Stir-Fried Broccoli with Tempeh and Lemon Threads

DAY SIX

Breakfast Juice:	Apple Sprout Juice 1 scoop protein powder (optional)
Breakfast:	Cream of Rice with Peaches and Honey
Snack:	1 Date Fudge Brownie
Lunch:	Gingery Bean Soup and Curried Waldorf Salad
Snack:	Tangy Carrot Dip with raw vegetables
Dinner Juice:	Cranberry Ginger Tonic
Dinner:	Mushroom Lasagna

DAY SEVEN

Breakfast Juice:	Celery Apple Juice 1 scoop protein powder (optional)
Breakfast:	Cocoa Kasha with Bananas
Snack:	Apple Pecan Cobbler
Lunch:	Curried Red Lentil Stew and Caesar Salad with Thyme Croutons
Snack:	Tomato Salsa with chips
Dinner Juice:	Romaine Lemon Tonic
Dinner:	Zesty Cauliflower with Garlic and Tahini and Peas Pillau with Cinnamon

Gary Null's Natural-Living Weight-Loss Tips

1. *Stop* being a couch potato.

Start being more active.

Exert more energy—use the stairs more, walk farther and for longer periods of time, and participate in more sports. Gradually establish a regular exercise routine involving running, cycling, or another aerobic activity.

2. *Stop* procrastinating.

Start getting things done.

Finishing things that you have been putting off will make you feel better about yourself and help keep your mind off food. Take up a cause, hobby, project, or even a new romance that renews your interest in life and makes you want to get up in the morning.

3. *Stop* being passive.

Start taking charge of your life.

Using food for comfort and reward is inappropriate, and soothing your sorrows and frustrations with fattening foods may actually deepen your depression. Instead of overeating, analyze what is bothering you, and take steps to eliminate the problem.

4. *Stop* punishing yourself with food.

Start accepting yourself for what you are.

Food is generally thought of as being pleasurable, but you might subconsciously be using food to punish yourself. Secretly, you may believe that you don't deserve to be pretty, popular, happy, or healthy. Stop being so hard on yourself, and start loving who you really are.

5. *Stop* setting idealistic long-term goals that are difficult to achieve.

Start setting realistic short-term goals that you can reach.

Whether the long-term goal is losing 10 pounds in one month or losing 100 pounds in one year, you are sure to run into temporary plateaus and disappointments—disappointments that could discourage you from continuing your efforts. It is better to set goals day-by-day or week-by-week. Then, if you make a mistake, you can forget it and move on to the next goal.

6. *Stop* isolating yourself.

Start seeing people.

Seeing people will help get your mind off food and end the depressing isolation you may impose on yourself when you feel fat and unattractive. Don't think you have to go it alone. If necessary, get help from a counselor or support group.

7. *Stop* thinking of yourself as dieting, starving, or deprived.

Start realizing that you are permanently changing your life for the better.

Generally, diets do not work. Most people regain lost weight in a dangerous diet yo-yo syndrome. Accept the fact that the healthy dietary changes you are making are *permanent.*

8. *Stop* putting food at the center of your life.

Start expanding your life in new areas.

Minimize the role of food in your social life. Join friends for sports or a movie rather than lunch. Find pleasurable activities other than meals to share with your family.

9. *Stop* thinking that you have to eat when and what the people around you are eating.

Start eating only when you should eat and only what is good for you.

If the three square meals a day your family eats are causing you unnecessary weight gain, don't eat them, *even if it means not eating with or cooking for your family.* You may need six small snacks a day to avoid the hunger pains that sometimes plague meal-stretched stomachs.

10. *Stop* eating fats, animal products, and "empty calories" (sugar, refined carbohydrates, alcohol, etc.).

Start eating more vegetables, fruits, and whole grains.

Losing weight has less to do with counting calories than with eating right. Vegetables, fruits, and whole grains not only help you lose weight, but also make you healthier because of their high vitamin, mineral, and fiber contents.

Vegetarian's Vocabulary

Arugula. A dark green, somewhat bitter lettuce, commonly used in salads.

Barley. A grain that while lower in fiber than other grains, is one of the easiest to digest. In a process called "pearling," barley's tough outer hull, which is almost impossible to digest, is removed.

Basil. An herb with bright green, pungent leaves. Basil is commonly used in Italian dishes.

Basmati Rice. A variety of Indian-grown rice with a distinctive nutty flavor and a light, fluffy texture.

Blackstrap Molasses. A rich, deep-brown sweetener that is the by-product of the process through which sugar cane is converted into refined sugar. Blackstrap molasses contains 35 percent sucrose, and is a good source of iron, calcium, and the B vitamins.

Buckwheat Flour. A dark, finely ground, highly nutritious flour made from the seeds of a plant native to Asia.

Bulghur wheat. A grain made from whole wheat that has been cracked, parboiled, and dried. Because of the parboiling, bulghur wheat can be prepared quickly.

Canola Oil. The mild-flavored oil extracted from the rapeseed.

Cardamom. An aromatic spice made by grinding the small, dark pods of a tropical plant native to Asia.

Carob. A rich-tasting dark brown powder made from the dried pods of a Mediterranean evergreen tree. Naturally sweet, carob powder can be used as is, or in the form of carob chips, and is a healthful alternative to chocolate.

Celery Seeds. Small, light brown, aromatic seeds that come from the wild celery plant.

Cilantro. The pungent, parsley-like leaves of the coriander plant.

Cocoa Powder. A powder made by roasting and grinding cacao seeds, and removing most of their oil.

Coriander. A spice made from the dried ripe seeds of the coriander plant. Coriander is commonly used in Asian dishes.

Cream of Brown Rice. A whole-grain cereal that must be cooked before eating. Cream of brown rice can be purchased in health-food stores.

Date Sugar. A natural sweetener made of dehydrated ground dates.

Extract. A concentrated flavoring made by combining alcohol with the oil extracted from almonds, lemons, vanilla, etc.

Garbanzo Beans (Chickpeas). A bean originally cultivated in the Middle East, where it is still considered a staple food item. Garbanzo beans—also called chickpeas and ceci—are used to make hummus, falafel, meatless loaves, dressings, and breads. They are also a popular addition to salads.

Kasha. Toasted buckwheat, also called buckwheat groats.

Lentils. Tasty beans that are a good source of protein, vitamin A, thiamin, riboflavin, niacin, iron, calcium, phosphorus, and potassium.

Maple Syrup. A natural sweetener with a rich flavor made by collecting and boiling the sap of maple trees until the sap becomes thick and sweet.

Millet. A light, fluffy, mild-tasting grain that is high in protein and well tolerated by people who are allergic to other grains. Only hulled millet is suitable for cooking.

Miso. A savory paste made from fermented soybeans. Miso is used mainly as a base for soups and sauces.

Nut Butter. A spread made by grinding raw or roasted nuts until the nuts have a creamy, spreadable consistency. While the best-known variety is peanut butter, nut butter can be made with any type of nut, including almonds, pecans, and walnuts.

Pine Nuts. The edible seeds from certain pines. Also known as Pignola and Indian nuts, these small, tasty nuts are low in protein and high in calories. Pine nuts are sometimes used as a vegetable or dessert garnish, and can also be used in the making of pesto.

Protein Powder. A dietary supplement commonly consisting of rice, sesame seeds, egg whites, and soy blends. Protein powder is high in protein, complex carbohydrates, and fiber, and is rich in essential vitamins and minerals.

Quinoa. Quick-cooking grains with a delicious, mild flavor. Quinoa is higher in protein, calcium, and iron than any other grain.

Radicchio. A red-colored, strong-flavored lettuce-like vegetable that is frequently used in salads.

Rice Syrup. A thick sweetener made from rice, sometimes with the addition of barley malt. Rice syrup is available in Oriental food markets and most health-food stores.

Safflower Oil. The oil extracted from the safflower plant, which belongs to the sunflower family. Probably the lightest and least flavorful of the cooking oils, safflower oil is 94 percent unsaturated.

Saffron Threads. The dried stigmas of the plant *crocus sativus*. Saffron is used as a food coloring and a cooking spice.

Sea Salt. The salt obtained from evaporated sea water (either from sun or kiln baking). Sea salt is high in trace vitamins and minerals, and contains no chemical additives.

Sesame Oil. The oil extracted from sesame seeds. The dark variety, obtained from seeds that were roasted before pressing, has a smoky flavor. The light variety, obtained from unroasted seeds, has a milder flavor. Hot sesame oil contains red pepper. Sesame oil is 87 percent unsaturated.

Sesame Seeds. Obtained from the sesame plant, these seeds are an excellent source of protein, unsaturated fatty acids, calcium, magnesium, niacin, and vitamins A and E.

Shiitake Mushrooms. Primarily grown in a special area of Japan, these mushrooms are used to flavor soup stocks and vegetable dishes.

Silken Tofu. A soft, creamy variety of tofu.

Soymilk. A non-dairy milk made from soybean mash. Soymilk contains no cholesterol.

Sprouts. Seeds that have begun to germinate. Sprouts are an excellent source of protein, and contain high levels of vitamins A, B, and E. Common sprouts include alfalfa, lentil, mung bean, and sunflower.

Sunflower Oil. The oil extracted from the seeds of the sunflower. Although similar in taste to safflower oil, sunflower oil is slightly stronger in flavor. This oil is 92 percent unsaturated.

Sunflower Seeds. The edible seeds of the sun-flower. These seeds are a rich source of protein, unsaturated fatty acids, phosphorus, calcium, iron, fluorine, iodine, potassium, magnesium, and zinc. Vitamin D and E and some of the B vitamins are also found in sunflower seeds.

Sweet Rice Vinegar. A traditional Japanese vine-gar made from fermented rice.

Tahini. A paste made by grinding hulled, un-roasted sesame seeds. Tahini is high in fat, protein, and calcium.

Tamari. Naturally fermented soy sauce. Tamari is a by-product of traditional miso-making. Easy to digest, tamari contains B vitamins, riboflavin, and niacin.

Tempeh. A fermented soybean product. Tempeh is high in protein, and is the richest vegetable source of vitamin B_{12}.

Tofu. A white, cheeselike product made from soy-bean curds. Mild-tasting tofu is high in protein, low in fat and calories, and rich in calcium.

Turmeric. A yellow-orange aromatic spice used in many Asian dishes.

Wheat Germ. The central base of the wheat kernel. Wheat germ is a rich source of both vitamin E and the B vitamins.

Nutrient Composition of Foods

In each of the tables that follow, the portion listed is 100 grams, which is roughly equal to 3 ounces.

APPLES, Raw, with skin

Nutrients and units	Amount in 100 grams, edible portion	Amount in edible portion of common measures of food	
	Mean	Approximate measure and weight	
		1 fruit = 138 g	1 c slices = 110 g
A	B	E	F
PROXIMATE:			
Water . . . . .g	83.93	115.83	92.33
Food energy . . . . { kcal	59	81	64
{ kj	245	338	270
Protein (N x 6.25) . . . . .g	0.19	0.27	0.21
Total lipid (fat) . . . . .g	0.36	0.49	0.39
Carbohydrate, total . . . . .g	15.25	21.05	16.78
Fiber . . . . .g	0.77	1.06	0.84
Ash . . . . .g	0.26	0.36	0.29
MINERALS:			
Calcium . . . . .mg	7	10	8
Iron . . . . .mg	0.18	0.25	0.20
Magnesium . . . . .mg	5	6	5
Phosphorus . . . . .mg	7	10	8
Potassium . . . . .mg	115	159	126
Sodium . . . . .mg	0	1	0
Zinc . . . . .mg	0.04	0.05	0.04
Copper .mg	0.041	0.057	0.045
Manganese . . . . .mg	0.045	0.062	0.050
VITAMINS:			
Ascorbic acid . . . . .mg	5.7	7.8	6.2
Thiamin . . . . .mg	0.017	0.023	0.019
Riboflavin . . . . .mg	0.014	0.019	0.015
Niacin . . . . .mg	0.077	0.106	0.085
Pantothenic acid . . . . .mg	0.061	0.084	0.067
Vitamin B₆ . . . . .mg	0.048	0.066	0.053
Folacin . . . . .mcg	2.8	3.9	3.1
Vitamin B₁₂ . . . . .mcg	0	0	0
Vitamin A . . . . { RE	5	7	6
{ IU	53	74	59

APPLES, Raw, without skin

Nutrients and units	Amount in 100 grams, edible portion	Amount in edible portion of common measures of food	
	Mean	Approximate measure and weight	
		1 fruit = 128 g	1 c slices = 110 g
A	B	E	F
PROXIMATE:			
Water . . . . .g	84.46	108.10	92.90
Food energy . . . . { kcal	57	72	62
{ kj	237	303	260
Protein (N x 6.25) . . . . .g	0.15	0.19	0.16
Total lipid (fat) . . . . .g	0.31	0.40	0.34
Carbohydrate, total . . . . .g	14.84	19.00	16.33
Fiber . . . . .g	0.54	0.69	0.59
Ash . . . . .g	0.24	0.31	0.27
MINERALS:			
Calcium . . . . .mg	4	5	4
Iron . . . . .mg	0.07	0.09	0.08
Magnesium . . . . .mg	3	4	3
Phosphorus . . . . .mg	7	9	8
Potassium . . . . .mg	113	144	124
Sodium .mg	0	0	0
Zinc . . . . .mg	0.04	0.05	0.04
Copper .mg	0.031	0.040	0.034
Manganese . . . . .mg	0.023	0.029	0.025
VITAMINS:			
Ascorbic acid . . . . .mg	4.0	5.1	4.4
Thiamin . . . . .mg	0.017	0.022	0.019
Riboflavin . . . . .mg	0.010	0.013	0.011
Niacin . . . . .mg	0.091	0.116	0.100
Pantothenic acid . . . . .mg	0.057	0.073	0.063
Vitamin B_6 . . . . .mg	0.046	0.059	0.051
Folacin . . . . .mcg	0.4	0.5	0.4
Vitamin B_{12} . . . . .mcg	0	0	0
Vitamin A . . . . { RE	4	6	5
{ IU	44	56	40

AVOCADOS, Raw, Florida

Nutrients and units	Amount in 100 grams, edible portion	Amount in edible portion of common measures of food	
	Mean	Approximate measure and weight	
		1 fruit = 304 g	1 c puree = 230 g
A	B	E	F
PROXIMATE:			
Water . . . . .g	79.73	242.39	183.39
Food energy . . . . { kcal	112	339	257
{ kj	467	1,420	1,074
Protein (N x 6.25) . . . . .g	1.59	4.83	3.65
Total lipid (fat) . . . . .g	8.87	26.95	20.39
Carbohydrate, total . . . . .g	8.91	27.09	20.50
Fiber . . . . .g	2.11	6.41	4.85
Ash . . . . .g	0.90	2.74	2.07
MINERALS:			
Calcium . . . . .mg	11	33	25
Iron . . . . .mg	0.53	1.60	1.21
Magnesium . . . . .mg	34	104	78
Phosphorus . . . . .mg	39	119	90
Potassium . . . . .mg	488	1,484	1,122
Sodium .mg	5	14	11
Zinc . . . . .mg	0.42	1.28	0.97
Copper .mg	0.251	0.763	0.577
Manganese . . . . .mg	0.170	0.517	0.391
VITAMINS:			
Ascorbic acid . . . . .mg	7.9	24.0	18.2
Thiamin . . . . .mg	0.108	0.328	0.248
Riboflavin . . . . .mg	0.122	0.371	0.281
Niacin . . . . .mg	1.921	5.840	4.418
Pantothenic acid . . . . .mg	0.971	2.952	2.233
Vitamin B_6 . . . . .mg	0.280	0.851	0.644
Folacin . . . . .mcg	53.3	161.9	122.5
Vitamin B_{12} . . . . .mcg	0	0	0
Vitamin A . . . . { RE	61	186	141
{ IU	612	1,860	1,407

BANANAS, Raw

Nutrients and units	Amount in 100 grams, edible portion	Amount in edible portion of common measures of food	
	Mean	Approximate measure and weight	
		1 fruit = 114 g	1 c mashed = 225 g
A	B	E	F
PROXIMATE:			
Water . . . . g	74.26	84.66	167.08
Food energy . . . . { kcal	92	105	207
{ kj	384	438	864
Protein (N x 6.25) . . . . g	1.03	1.18	2.32
Total lipid (fat) . . . . g	0.48	0.55	1.08
Carbohydrate, total . . . . g	23.43	26.71	52.71
Fiber . . . . g	0.50	0.57	1.13
Ash . . . . g	0.80	0.91	1.80
MINERALS:			
Calcium . . . . mg	6	7	13
Iron . . . . mg	0.31	0.35	0.69
Magnesium . . . . mg	29	33	64
Phosphorus . . . . mg	20	22	44
Potassium . . . . mg	396	451	890
Sodium . . . . mg	1	1	2
Zinc . . . . mg	0.16	0.19	0.37
Copper . . . . mg	0.104	0.119	0.234
Manganese . . . . mg	0.152	0.173	0.342
VITAMINS:			
Ascorbic acid . . . . mg	9.1	10.3	20.4
Thiamin . . . . mg	0.045	0.051	0.101
Riboflavin . . . . mg	0.100	0.114	0.225
Niacin . . . . mg	0.540	0.616	1.215
Pantothenic acid . . . . mg	0.260	0.296	0.585
Vitamin B$_6$ . . . . mg	0.578	0.659	1.301
Folacin . . . . mcg	19.1	21.8	43.0
Vitamin B$_{12}$ . . . . mcg	0	0	0
Vitamin A . . . . { RE	8	9	18
{ IU	81	92	182

BLACKBERRIES, Raw

Nutrients and units	Amount in 100 grams, edible portion	Amount in edible portion of common measures of food	
		Approximate measure and weight	
	Mean	½ c = 72 g	1 c = 144 g
A	B	E	F
PROXIMATE:			
Water ....g	85.64	61.66	123.33
Food energy .... { kcal	52	37	74
{ kj	216	156	311
Protein (N x 6.25) ....g	0.72	0.52	1.04
Total lipid (fat) ....g	0.39	0.28	0.56
Carbohydrate, total ....g	12.76	9.19	18.38
Fiber ....g	4.10	2.95	5.90
Ash ....g	0.48	0.35	0.70
MINERALS:			
Calcium ....mg	32	23	46
Iron ....mg	0.57	0.41	0.83
Magnesium ....mg	20	14	29
Phosphorus..................mg	21	15	30
Potassium ....mg	196	141	282
Sodium ....mg	0	0	0
Zinc ....mg	0.27	0.20	0.39
Copper ....mg	0.140	0.101	0.202
Manganese ....mg	1.291	0.930	1.859
VITAMINS:			
Ascorbic acid................mg	21.0	15.1	30.2
Thiamin ....mg	0.030	0.022	0.043
Riboflavin ....mg	0.040	0.029	0.058
Niacin......................mg	0.400	0.288	0.576
Pantothenic acid ....mg	0.240	0.173	0.346
Vitamin B₆ ....mg	0.058	0.042	0.084
Folacin ....mcg			
Vitamin B₁₂ ....mcg	0	0	0
Vitamin A.................. { RE	16	12	24
{ IU	165	119	237

BLUEBERRIES, Raw

Nutrients and units	Amount in 100 grams, edible portion	Amount in edible portion of common measures of food	
		Approximate measure and weight	
	Mean	1 c = 145 g	1 pint = 402 g
A	B	E	F
PROXIMATE:			
Water ....g	84.61	122.68	340.13
Food energy .... { kcal	56	82	226
{ kj	236	342	947
Protein (N x 6.25) ....g	0.67	0.97	2.69
Total lipid (fat) ....g	0.38	0.55	1.53
Carbohydrate, total ....g	14.13	20.49	56.81
Fiber ....g	1.30	1.88	5.21
Ash ....g	0.21	0.30	0.84
MINERALS:			
Calcium ....mg	6	9	25
Iron ....mg	0.17	0.24	0.66
Magnesium ....mg	5	7	20
Phosphorus..................mg	10	15	41
Potassium ....mg	89	129	357
Sodium ....mg	6	9	24
Zinc ....mg	0.11	0.160	0.43
Copper ....mg	0.061	0.088	0.245
Manganese ....mg	0.282	0.409	1.134
VITAMINS:			
Ascorbic acid................mg	13.0	18.9	52.3
Thiamin ....mg	0.048	0.070	0.193
Riboflavin ....mg	0.050	0.073	0.201
Niacin......................mg	0.359	0.521	1.443
Pantothenic acid ....mg	0.093	0.135	0.374
Vitamin B₆ ....mg	0.036	0.052	0.145
Folacin ....mcg	6.400	9.3	25.7
Vitamin B₁₂ ....mcg	0	0	0
Vitamin A.................. { RE	10	15	40
{ IU	100	145	402

CHERRIES, Sweet, raw

Nutrients and units	Amount in 100 grams, edible portion	Amount in edible portion of common measures of food	
	Mean	Approximate measure and weight	
		10 fruits = 68 g	1 c = 145 g
A	B	E	F
PROXIMATE:			
Water . . . . .g	80.76	54.91	117.09
Food energy . . . . { kcal	72	49	104
kj	300	204	435
Protein (N x 6.25) . . . . .g	1.20	0.82	1.74
Total lipid (fat) . . . . .g	0.96	0.65	1.39
Carbohydrate, total . . . . .g	16.55	11.25	24.00
Fiber . . . . .g	0.40	0.27	0.58
Ash . . . . .g	0.53	0.36	0.77
MINERALS:			
Calcium .mg	15	10	21
Iron . . . . .mg	0.39	0.26	0.56
Magnesium . . . . .mg	11	8	16
Phosphorus . . . . .mg	19	13	28
Potassium . . . . .mg	224	152	325
Sodium . . . . .mg	0	0	1
Zinc . . . . .mg	0.06	0.04	0.09
Copper . . . . .mg	0.095	0.065	0.138
Manganese . . . . .mg	0.092	0.063	0.133
VITAMINS:			
Ascorbic acid . . . . .mg	7.0	4.8	10.2
Thiamin .mg	0.050	0.034	0.073
Riboflavin . . . . .mg	0.060	0.041	0.087
Niacin . . . . .mg	0.400	0.272	0.580
Pantothenic acid . . . . .mg	0.127	0.086	0.184
Vitamin B$_6$ . . . . .mg	0.036	0.024	0.052
Folacin .mcg	4.2	2.8	6.1
Vitamin B$_{12}$ . . . . .mcg	0	0	0
Vitamin A . . . . { RE	21	15	31
IU	214	146	310

GRAPEFRUIT, Raw, pink, red, and white, all areas

Nutrients and units	Amount in 100 grams, edible portion	Amount in edible portion of common measures of food	
	Mean	Approximate measure and weight	
		½ fruit = 120 g	1 c sections with juice = 230 g
A	B	E	F
PROXIMATE:			
Water . . . . .g	90.89	109.06	209.04
Food energy . . . . { kcal	32	38	74
kj	134	161	308
Protein (N x 6.25) . . . . .g	0.63	0.75	1.45
Total lipid (fat) . . . . .g	0.10	0.12	0.23
Carbohydrate, total . . . . .g	8.08	9.70	18.58
Fiber . . . . .g	0.20	0.24	0.46
Ash . . . . .g	0.31	0.37	0.71
MINERALS:			
Calcium .mg	12	14	27
Iron . . . . .mg	0.09	0.10	0.20
Magnesium . . . . .mg	8	10	19
Phosphorus . . . . .mg	8	10	20
Potassium . . . . .mg	139	167	321
Sodium . . . . .mg	0	0	1
Zinc . . . . .mg	0.07	0.09	0.16
Copper . . . . .mg	0.047	0.056	0.108
Manganese . . . . .mg	0.012	0.014	0.028
VITAMINS:			
Ascorbic acid . . . . .mg	34.4	41.3	79.1
Thiamin .mg	0.036	0.043	0.083
Riboflavin . . . . .mg	0.020	0.024	0.046
Niacin . . . . .mg	0.250	0.300	0.575
Pantothenic acid . . . . .mg	0.283	0.340	0.651
Vitamin B$_6$ . . . . .mg	0.042	0.050	0.097
Folacin .mcg	10.2	12.2	23.4
Vitamin B$_{12}$ . . . . .mcg	0	0	0
Vitamin A . . . . { RE	12	15	29
IU	124	149	286

GRAPES, American type (slip skin), raw

Nutrients and units	Amount in 100 grams, edible portion	Amount in edible portion of common measures of food	
	Mean	Approximate measure and weight	
		10 fruits = 24 g	1 c = 92 g
A	B	E	F
PROXIMATE:			
Water . . . . .g	81.30	19.51	74.80
Food energy { kcal	63	16	58
kj	263	63	242
Protein (N x 6.25) . . . . .g	0.63	0.15	0.58
Total lipid (fat) . . . . .g	0.35	0.08	0.32
Carbohydrate, total . . . . .g	17.15	4.12	15.78
Fiber . . . . .g	0.76	0.18	0.70
Ash . . . . .g	0.57	0.14	0.52
MINERALS:			
Calcium . . . . .mg	14	3	13
Iron .mg	0.29	0.07	0.27
Magnesium . . . . .mg	5	1	5
Phosphorus . . . . .mg	10	2	9
Potassium . . . . .mg	191	46	176
Sodium . . . . .mg	2	0	2
Zinc .mg	0.04	0.01	0.04
Copper . . . . .mg	0.040	0.010	0.037
Manganese . . . . .mg	0.718	0.172	0.661
VITAMINS:			
Ascorbic acid . . . . .mg	4.0	1.0	3.7
Thiamin . . . . .mg	0.092	0.022	0.085
Riboflavin . . . . .mg	0.057	0.014	0.052
Niacin .mg	0.300	0.072	0.276
Pantothenic acid . . . . .mg	0.024	0.006	0.022
Vitamin B_6 . . . . .mg	0.110	0.026	0.101
Folacin . . . . .mcg	3.9	0.9	3.6
Vitamin B_{12} . . . . .mcg	0	0	0
Vitamin A . . . . { RE	10	2	9
IU	100	24	92

GRAPES, European type (adherent skin), raw

Nutrients and units	Amount in 100 grams, edible portion	Amount in edible portion of common measures of food	
	Mean	Approximate measure and weight	
		10 fruits = 50 g	1 c = 160 g
A	B	E	F
PROXIMATE:			
Water . . . . .g	80.56	40.28	128.90
Food energy { kcal	71	36	114
kj	297	149	475
Protein (N x 6.25) . . . . .g	0.66	0.33	1.06
Total lipid (fat) . . . . .g	0.58	0.29	0.92
Carbohydrate, total . . . . .g	17.77	8.88	28.43
Fiber . . . . .g	0.45	0.23	0.72
Ash . . . . .g	0.44	0.22	0.70
MINERALS:			
Calcium . . . . .mg	11	5	17
Iron .mg	0.26	0.13	0.41
Magnesium . . . . .mg	6	3	10
Phosphorus . . . . .mg	13	6	21
Potassium . . . . .mg	185	93	296
Sodium . . . . .mg	2	1	3
Zinc .mg	0.05	0.03	0.09
Copper . . . . .mg	0.090	0.045	0.144
Manganese . . . . .mg	0.058	0.029	0.093
VITAMINS:			
Ascorbic acid . . . . .mg	10.8	5.4	17.3
Thiamin . . . . .mg	0.092	0.046	0.147
Riboflavin . . . . .mg	0.057	0.029	0.091
Niacin .mg	0.300	0.150	0.480
Pantothenic acid . . . . .mg	0.024	0.012	0.038
Vitamin B_6 . . . . .mg	0.110	0.055	0.176
Folacin . . . . .mcg	3.9	2.0	6.3
Vitamin B_{12} . . . . .mcg	0	0	0
Vitamin A . . . . { RE	7	4	12
IU	73	36	117

KIWIFRUIT, Raw

Nutrients and units	Amount in 100 grams, edible portion	Amount in edible portion of common measures of food	
	Mean	Approximate measure and weight	
		1 medium fruit = 76 g	1 large fruit = 91 g
A	B	E	F
PROXIMATE:			
Water ....g	83.05	63.12	75.58
Food energy .... { kcal	61	46	55
{ kj	254	193	231
Protein (N x 6.25) ....g	0.99	0.75	0.90
Total lipid (fat) ....g	0.44	0.34	0.40
Carbohydrate, total ....g	14.88	11.31	13.54
Fiber ....g	1.10	0.84	1.00
Ash ....g	0.64	0.49	0.58
MINERALS:			
Calcium ....mg	26	20	24
Iron ....mg	0.41	0.31	0.37
Magnesium ....mg	30	23	27
Phosphorus ....mg	40	31	37
Potassium ....mg	332	252	302
Sodium ....mg	5	4	4
Zinc ....mg			
Copper ....mg			
Manganese ....mg			
VITAMINS:			
Ascorbic acid................mg	98.0	74.5	89.2
Thiamin ....mg	0.020	0.015	0.018
Riboflavin ....mg	0.050	0.038	0.046
Niacin ....mg	0.500	0.380	0.455
Pantothenic acid ....mg			
Vitamin B_6................. mg			
Folacin ....mcg			
Vitamin B_{12} ....mcg	0	0	0
Vitamin A................. { RE	18	13	16
{ IU	175	133	159

KUMQUATS, Raw

Nutrients and units	Amount in 100 grams, edible portion	Amount in edible portion of common measures of food
	Mean	Approximate measure and weight 1 fruit = 19 g
A	B	E	F

PROXIMATE:

Water ....g	81.70	15.52	
Food energy .... { kcal	63	12	
{ kj	264	50	
Protein (N x 6.25) ....g	0.90	0.17	
Total lipid (fat) ....g	0.10	0.02	
Carbohydrate, total ....g	16.43	3.12	
Fiber ....g	3.70	0.70	
Ash ....g	0.87	0.17	

MINERALS:

Calcium ....mg	44	8	
Iron ....mg	0.39	0.07	
Magnesium ....mg	13	2	
Phosphorus ....mg	19	4	
Potassium ....mg	195	37	
Sodium ....mg	6	1	
Zinc ....mg	0.08	0.02	
Copper ....mg	0.107	0.020	
Manganese ....mg	0.086	0.016	

VITAMINS:

Ascorbic acid................mg	37.4	7.1	
Thiamin ....mg	0.080	0.015	
Riboflavin ....mg	0.100	0.019	
Niacin ....mg			
Pantothenic acid ....mg			
Vitamin B6 ....mg			
Folacin ....mcg			
Vitamin B12 ....mcg	0	0	
Vitamin A.................. { RE	30	6	
{ IU	302	57	

LEMONS, Raw, without peel

Nutrients and units	Amount in 100 grams, edible portion	Amount in edible portion of common measures of food	
	Mean	Approximate measure and weight 1 medium fruit = 58 g	1 large fruit = 84 g
A	B	E	F

PROXIMATE:

Water ....g	88.98	51.61	74.74
Food energy .... { kcal	29	17	25
{ kj	123	71	103
Protein (N x 6.25) ....g	1.10	0.64	0.92
Total lipid (fat) ....g	0.30	0.17	0.25
Carbohydrate, total ....g	9.32	5.41	7.83
Fiber ....g	0.40	0.23	0.34
Ash ....g	0.30	0.17	0.25

MINERALS:

Calcium ....mg	26	15	22
Iron ....mg	0.60	0.35	0.50
Magnesium ....mg			
Phosphorus ....mg	16	9	13
Potassium ....mg	138	80	116
Sodium ....mg	2	1	2
Zinc ....mg	0.06	0.04	0.05
Copper ....mg	0.037	0.021	0.031
Manganese ....mg			

VITAMINS:

Ascorbic acid................mg	53.0	30.7	44.5
Thiamin ....mg	0.040	0.023	0.034
Riboflavin ....mg	0.020	0.012	0.017
Niacin ....mg	0.100	0.058	0.084
Pantothenic acid ....mg	0.190	0.110	0.160
Vitamin B6 ....mg	0.080	0.046	0.067
Folacin ....mcg	10.6	6.2	8.9
Vitamin B12 ....mcg	0	0	0
Vitamin A.................. { RE	3	2	2
{ IU	29	17	24

MELONS, Cantaloup, raw

Nutrients and units	Amount in 100 grams, edible portion	Amount in edible portion of common measures of food	
	Mean	½ fruit = 267 g	1 c cubed pieces = 160 g
A	B	E	F
PROXIMATE:			
Water ....g	89.78	239.71	143.64
Food energy { kcal	35	94	57
{ kJ	148	395	237
Protein (N x 6.25).............g	0.88	2.34	1.40
Total lipid (fat) ....g	0.28	0.74	0.44
Carbohydrate, total ....g	8.36	22.33	13.38
Fiber ....g	0.36	0.97	0.58
Ash ....g	0.71	1.88	1.13
MINERALS:			
Calcium ....mg	11	28	17
Iron ....mg	0.21	0.57	0.34
Magnesium ....mg	11	28	17
Phosphorus................mg	17	45	27
Potassium ....mg	309	825	494
Sodium ....mg	9	23	14
Zinc ....mg	0.16	0.41	0.25
Copper ....mg	0.042	0.112	0.067
Manganese ....mg	0.047	0.125	0.075
VITAMINS:			
Ascorbic acid...............mg	42.2	112.7	67.5
Thiamin ....mg	0.036	0.096	0.058
Riboflavin ....mg	0.021	0.056	0.034
Niacin....................mg	0.574	1.533	0.918
Pantothenic acid ....mg	0.128	0.342	0.205
Vitamin B_6...................mg	0.115	0.307	0.184
Folacin ....mcg	17.0	45.5	27.3
Vitamin B_{12} ....mcg	0	0	0
Vitamin A.............. { RE	322	861	516
{ IU	3,224	8,608	5,158

MELONS, Casaba, raw

Nutrients and units	Amount in 100 grams, edible portion	Amount in edible portion of common measures of food	
	Mean	1/10 fruit = 164 g	1 c cubed pieces = 170 g
A	B	E	F
PROXIMATE:			
Water ....g	92.00	150.88	156.40
Food energy { kcal	26	43	45
{ kJ	110	180	186
Protein (N x 6.25).............g	0.90	1.48	1.53
Total lipid (fat) ....g	0.10	0.16	0.17
Carbohydrate, total ....g	6.20	10.17	10.54
Fiber ....g	0.50	0.82	0.85
Ash ....g	0.80	1.31	1.36
MINERALS:			
Calcium ....mg	5	8	9
Iron ....mg	0.40	0.66	0.68
Magnesium ....mg	8	13	14
Phosphorus................mg	7	11	12
Potassium ....mg	210	344	357
Sodium ....mg	12	20	20
Zinc ....mg			
Copper ....mg			
Manganese ....mg			
VITAMINS:			
Ascorbic acid...............mg	16.0	26.2	27.2
Thiamin ....mg	0.060	0.098	0.102
Riboflavin ....mg	0.020	0.033	0.034
Niacin....................mg	0.400	0.656	0.680
Pantothenic acid ....mg			
Vitamin B_6...................mg			
Folacin ....mcg			
Vitamin B_{12} ....mcg	0	0	0
Vitamin A.............. { RE	3	5	5
{ IU	30	49	51

MELONS, Honeydew, raw

Nutrients and units	Amount in 100 grams, edible portion	Amount in edible portion of common measures of food	
	Mean	Approximate measure and weight	
		1/10 fruit = 129 g	1 c cubed pieces = 170 g
A	B	E	F
PROXIMATE:			
Water . . . . g	89.66	115.66	152.43
Food energy . . . . { kcal	35	46	60
{ kj	148	191	252
Protein (N x 6.25) . . . . g	0.46	0.59	0.77
Total lipid (fat) . . . . g	0.10	0.13	0.17
Carbohydrate, total . . . . g	9.18	11.84	15.61
Fiber . . . . g	0.60	0.77	1.02
Ash . . . . g	0.60	0.78	1.02
MINERALS:			
Calcium . . . . mg	6	8	10
Iron . . . . mg	0.07	0.09	0.12
Magnesium . . . . mg	7	9	12
Phosphorus . . . . mg	10	13	17
Potassium . . . . mg	271	350	461
Sodium . . . . mg	10	13	17
Zinc . . . . mg			
Copper . . . . mg	0.041	0.053	0.070
Manganese . . . . mg	0.018	0.023	0.031
VITAMINS:			
Ascorbic acid . . . . mg	24.8	32.0	42.1
Thiamin . . . . mg	0.077	0.099	0.131
Riboflavin . . . . mg	0.018	0.023	0.031
Niacin . . . . mg	0.600	0.774	1.020
Pantothenic acid . . . . mg	0.207	0.267	0.352
Vitamin B_6 . . . . mg	0.059	0.076	0.100
Folacin . . . . mcg			
Vitamin B_{12} . . . . mcg	0	0	0
Vitamin A . . . . { RE	4	5	7
{ IU	40	52	68

NECTARINES, Raw

Nutrients and units	Amount in 100 grams, edible portion	Amount in edible portion of common measures of food	
	Mean	Approximate measure and weight	
		1 fruit = 136 g	1 c slices = 138 g
A	B	E	F
PROXIMATE:			
Water .g	86.28	117.34	119.06
Food energy { kcal	49	67	68
Food energy { kj	207	281	285
Protein (N x 6.25) . . . . .g	0.94	1.28	1.30
Total lipid (fat) . . . . .g	0.46	0.62	0.63
Carbohydrate, total . . . . .g	11.78	16.03	16.26
Fiber . . . . .g	0.40	0.54	0.55
Ash . . . . .g	0.54	0.74	0.75
MINERALS:			
Calcium . . . . .mg	5	6	6
Iron . . . . .mg	0.15	0.21	0.21
Magnesium . . . . .mg	8	11	11
Phosphorus . . . . .mg	16	22	22
Potassium . . . . .mg	212	288	292
Sodium . . . . .mg	0	0	0
Zinc . . . . .mg	0.09	0.12	0.12
Copper . . . . .mg	0.073	0.099	0.101
Manganese . . . . .mg	0.044	0.060	0.061
VITAMINS:			
Ascorbic acid. . . . . .mg	5.4	7.3	7.4
Thiamin . . . . .mg	0.017	0.023	0.023
Riboflavin . . . . .mg	0.041	0.056	0.057
Niacin .mg	0.990	1.346	1.366
Pantothenic acid . . . . .mg	0.158	0.215	0.218
Vitamin B6 . . . . .mg	0.025	0.034	0.035
Folacin . . . . .mcg	3.7	5.1	5.2
Vitamin B12 . . . . .mcg	0	0	0
Vitamin A. . . . . { RE	74	100	102
Vitamin A. . . . . { IU	736	1,001	1,016

ORANGES, Raw, California, Valencias

Nutrients and units	Amount in 100 grams, edible portion	Amount in edible portion of common measures of food	
	Mean	Approximate measure and weight	
		1 fruit = 121 g	1 c section without membrane = 180 g
A	B	E	F
PROXIMATE:			
Water .g	86.34	104.47	155.41
Food energy { kcal	49	59	88
Food energy { kj	205	248	369
Protein (N x 6.25) . . . . .g	1.04	1.26	1.87
Total lipid (fat) . . . . .g	0.30	0.36	0.54
Carbohydrate, total . . . . .g	11.89	14.39	21.40
Fiber . . . . .g	0.50	0.61	0.90
Ash . . . . .g	0.42	0.51	0.76
MINERALS:			
Calcium . . . . .mg	40	48	72
Iron . . . . .mg	0.09	0.11	0.16
Magnesium . . . . .mg	10	12	18
Phosphorus . . . . .mg	17	21	31
Potassium . . . . .mg	179	217	322
Sodium . . . . .mg	0	0	0
Zinc . . . . .mg	0.06	0.07	0.11
Copper . . . . .mg	0.037	0.045	0.067
Manganese . . . . .mg	0.023	0.028	0.041
VITAMINS:			
Ascorbic acid. . . . . .mg	48.5	58.7	87.3
Thiamin . . . . .mg	0.087	0.105	0.157
Riboflavin . . . . .mg	0.040	0.048	0.072
Niacin .mg	0.274	0.332	0.493
Pantothenic acid . . . . .mg	0.250	0.303	0.450
Vitamin B6 . . . . .mg	0.063	0.076	0.113
Folacin . . . . .mcg	38.6	46.7	69.5
Vitamin B12 . . . . .mcg	0	0	0
Vitamin A. . . . . { RE	23	28	41
Vitamin A. . . . . { IU	230	278	414

ORANGES, Raw, Florida

Nutrients and units	Amount in 100 grams, edible portion	Amount in edible portion of common measures of food	
	Mean	Approximate measure and weight	
		1 fruit = 151 g	1 c sections without membrane = 185 g
A	B	E	F
PROXIMATE:			
Water .g	87.14	131.58	161.21
Food energy { kcal	46	69	84
{ kj	191	289	354
Protein (N x 6.25) . . . . .g	0.70	1.06	1.30
Total lipid (fat) . . . . .g	0.21	0.32	0.39
Carbohydrate, total . . . . .g	11.54	17.42	21.34
Fiber . . . . .g	0.34	0.52	0.64
Ash . . . . .g	0.41	0.62	0.76
MINERALS:			
Calcium . . . . .mg	43	65	80
Iron . . . . .mg	0.09	0.13	0.16
Magnesium . . . . .mg	10	15	19
Phosphorus . . . . .mg	12	18	22
Potassium . . . . .mg	169	254	312
Sodium . . . . .mg	0	1	1
Zinc . . . . .mg	0.08	0.12	0.15
Copper . . . . .mg	0.039	0.059	0.072
Manganese . . . . .mg	0.024	0.036	0.044
VITAMINS:			
Ascorbic acid . . . . .mg	45.0	68.0	83.3
Thiamin . . . . .mg	0.100	0.151	0.185
Riboflavin . . . . .mg	0.040	0.060	0.074
Niacin .mg	0.400	0.604	0.740
Pantothenic acid . . . . .mg	0.250	0.378	0.463
Vitamin B_6 . . . . .mg	0.051	0.077	0.094
Folacin . . . . .mcg	17.3	26.1	32.0
Vitamin B_{12} . . . . .mcg	0	0	0
Vitamin A . . . . { RE	20	30	37
{ IU	200	302	370

ORANGE JUICE, Canned

Nutrients and units	Amount in 100 grams, edible portion	Amount in edible portion of common measures of food	
	Mean	Approximate measure and weight	
		1 fl oz = 31.1 g	1 c = 249 g
A	B	E	F
PROXIMATE:			
Water .g	89.01	27.68	221.63
Food energy { kcal	42	13	104
{ kj	175	54	435
Protein (N x 6.25) . . . . .g	0.59	0.18	1.46
Total lipid (fat) . . . . .g	0.14	0.04	0.36
Carbohydrate, total . . . . .g	9.85	3.06	24.51
Fiber . . . . .g	0.10	0.03	0.25
Ash . . . . .g	0.41	0.13	1.03
MINERALS:			
Calcium . . . . .mg	8	3	21
Iron . . . . .mg	0.44	0.14	1.10
Magnesium . . . . .mg	11	3	27
Phosphorus . . . . .mg	14	4	36
Potassium . . . . .mg	175	54	436
Sodium . . . . .mg	2	1	6
Zinc . . . . .mg	0.07	0.02	0.17
Copper . . . . .mg	0.057	0.018	0.142
Manganese . . . . .mg	0.014	0.004	0.035
VITAMINS:			
Ascorbic acid . . . . .mg	34.4	10.7	85.7
Thiamin . . . . .mg	0.060	0.019	0.149
Riboflavin . . . . .mg	0.028	0.009	0.070
Niacin .mg	0.314	0.098	0.782
Pantothenic acid . . . . .mg	0.150	0.047	0.374
Vitamin B_6 . . . . .mg	0.088	0.027	0.219
Folacin . . . . .mcg			
Vitamin B_{12} . . . . .mcg	0	0	0
Vitamin A . . . . { RE	18	5	44
{ IU	175	55	437

ORANGE JUICE, Chilled

Nutrients and units	Amount in 100 grams, edible portion	Amount in edible portion of common measures of food	
	Mean	Approximate measure and weight	
		1 fl oz = 31.1 g	1 c = 249 g
—A—	—B—	—E—	—F—
PROXIMATE:			
Water . . . . g	88.40	27.49	220.10
Food energy . . . . { kcal	44	14	110
kj	186	58	462
Protein (N x 6.25) . . . . g	0.80	0.25	2.00
Total lipid (fat) . . . . g	0.27	0.08	0.67
Carbohydrate, total . . . . g	10.06	3.13	25.04
Fiber . . . . g			
Ash . . . . g	0.48	0.15	1.19
MINERALS:			
Calcium . . . . mg	10	3	24
Iron . . . . mg	0.17	0.05	0.41
Magnesium . . . . mg	11	3	28
Phosphorus . . . . mg	11	4	28
Potassium . . . . mg	190	59	473
Sodium . . . . mg	1	0	2
Zinc . . . . mg	0.04	0.01	0.11
Copper . . . . mg	0.040	0.012	0.100
Manganese . . . . mg	0.023	0.007	0.057
VITAMINS:			
Ascorbic acid . . . . mg	32.9	10.2	81.9
Thiamin . . . . mg	0.111	0.035	0.276
Riboflavin . . . . mg	0.021	0.007	0.052
Niacin . . . . mg	0.280	0.087	0.697
Pantothenic acid . . . . mg	0.191	0.059	0.476
Vitamin B_6 . . . . mg	0.054	0.017	0.134
Folacin . . . . mcg	18.1	5.6	45.2
Vitamin B_{12} . . . . mcg	0	0	0
Vitamin A . . . . { RE	8	2	19
IU	78	24	194

PAPAYAS, Raw

Nutrients and units	Amount in 100 grams, edible portion	Amount in edible portion of common measures of food	
	Mean	Approximate measure and weight	
		1 fruit = 304 g	c cubed pieces = 140 g
—A—	—B—	—E—	—F—
PROXIMATE:			
Water . . . . g	88.83	270.04	124.36
Food energy . . . . { kcal	39	117	54
kj	161	490	226
Protein (N x 6.25) . . . . g	0.61	1.86	0.86
Total lipid (fat) . . . . g	0.14	0.43	0.20
Carbohydrate, total . . . . g	9.81	29.82	13.73
Fiber . . . . g	0.77	2.35	1.08
Ash . . . . g	0.61	1.85	0.85
MINERALS:			
Calcium . . . . mg	24	72	33
Iron . . . . mg	0.10	0.30	0.14
Magnesium . . . . mg	10	31	14
Phosphorus . . . . mg	5	16	7
Potassium . . . . mg	257	780	359
Sodium . . . . mg	3	8	4
Zinc . . . . mg	0.07	0.22	0.10
Copper . . . . mg	0.016	0.049	0.022
Manganese . . . . mg	0.011	0.033	0.015
VITAMINS:			
Ascorbic acid . . . . mg	61.8	187.8	86.5
Thiamin . . . . mg	0.027	0.082	0.038
Riboflavin . . . . mg	0.032	0.097	0.045
Niacin . . . . mg	0.338	1.028	0.473
Pantothenic acid . . . . mg	0.218	0.663	0.305
Vitamin B_6 . . . . mg	0.019	0.058	0.027
Folacin . . . . mcg			
Vitamin B_{12} . . . . mcg	0	0	0
Vitamin A . . . . { RE	201	612	282
IU	2,014	6,122	2,819

PAPAYA NECTAR, Canned

Nutrients and units	Amount in 100 grams, edible portion	Amount in edible portion of common measures of food	
	Mean	Approximate measure and weight 1 fl oz = 31.2 g	1 c = 250 g
A	B	E	F
PROXIMATE:			
Water . . . . .g	85.02	26.53	212.54
Food energy . . . . { kcal	57	18	142
kj	238	74	596
Protein (N x 6.25) . . . . .g	0.17	0.05	0.43
Total lipid (fat) . . . . .g	0.15	0.05	0.38
Carbohydrate, total . . . . .g	14.51	4.53	36.28
Fiber . . . . .g			
Ash . . . . .g	0.15	0.05	0.38
MINERALS:			
Calcium . . . . .mg	10	3	24
Iron .mg	0.34	0.11	0.86
Magnesium . . . . .mg	3	1	8
Phosphorus . . . . .mg	0	0	1
Potassium . . . . .mg	31	10	78
Sodium . . . . .mg	5	2	14
Zinc .mg	0.15	0.05	0.38
Copper . . . . .mg	0.013	0.004	0.033
Manganese . . . . .mg	0.013	0.004	0.033
VITAMINS:			
Ascorbic acid . . . . .mg	3.0	0.9	7.5
Thiamin . . . . .mg	0.006	0.002	0.015
Riboflavin . . . . .mg	0.004	0.001	0.010
Niacin . . . . .mg	0.150	0.047	0.375
Pantothenic acid . . . . .mg	0.054	0.017	0.135
Vitamin B$_6$ . . . . .mg	0.009	0.003	0.023
Folacin . . . . .mcg	2.1	0.6	5.2
Vitamin B$_{12}$ . . . . .mcg	0	0	0
Vitamin A . . . . { RE	11	3	28
IU	111	35	277

PASSION-FRUIT JUICE, Yellow, raw

Nutrients and units	Amount in 100 grams, edible portion	Amount in edible portion of common measures of food	
	Mean	Approximate measure and weight 1 fl oz. = 30.9 g	1 c = 247 g
A	B	E	F
PROXIMATE:			
Water . . . . .g	84.21	26.02	208.00
Food energy . . . . { kcal	60	19	149
kj.	253	78	624
Protein (N x 6.25) . . . . .g	0.67	0.21	1.65
Total lipid (fat) . . . . .g	0.18	0.06	0.44
Carbohydrate, total . . . . .g	14.45	4.47	35.69
Fiber . . . . .g	0.17	0.05	0.42
Ash . . . . .g	0.49	0.15	1.21
MINERALS:			
Calcium . . . . .mg	4	1	9
Iron .mg	0.36	0.11	0.89
Magnesium . . . . .mg	17	5	41
Phosphorus . . . . .mg	25	8	61
Potassium . . . . .mg	278	86	687
Sodium . . . . .mg	6	2	15
Zinc .mg			
Copper . . . . .mg			
Manganese . . . . .mg			
VITAMINS:			
Ascorbic acid . . . . .mg	18.2	5.6	45.0
Thiamin . . . . .mg			
Riboflavin . . . . .mg	0.101	0.031	0.249
Niacin . . . . .mg	2.240	0.692	5.533
Pantothenic acid . . . . .mg			
Vitamin B$_6$ . . . . .mg			
Folacin . . . . .mcg			
Vitamin B$_{12}$ . . . . .mcg	0	0	0
Vitamin A . . . . { RE	241	74	595
IU	2,410	745	5,953

PEACHES, Raw

Nutrients and units	Amount in 100 grams, edible portion	Amount in edible portion of common measures of food	
	Mean	Approximate measure and weight 1 fruit = 87 g	1 c slices = 170 g
A	B	E	F
PROXIMATE:			
Water . . . . .g	87.66	76.26	149.02
Food energy { kcal	43	37	73
kj	180	157	306
Protein (N x 6.25) . . . . .g	0.70	0.61	1.19
Total lipid (fat) . . . . .g	0.09	0.08	0.16
Carbohydrate, total . . . . .g	11.10	9.65	18.86
Fiber . . . . .g	0.64	0.56	1.09
Ash . . . . .g	0.46	0.40	0.78
MINERALS:			
Calcium .mg	5	5	9
Iron . . . . .mg	0.11	0.10	0.19
Magnesium . . . . .mg	7	6	11
Phosphorus . . . . .mg	12	11	21
Potassium . . . . .mg	197	171	334
Sodium . . . . .mg	0	0	1
Zinc . . . . .mg	0.14	0.12	0.23
Copper . . . . .mg	0.068	0.059	0.116
Manganese . . . . .mg	0.047	0.041	0.080
VITAMINS:			
Ascorbic acid . . . . .mg	6.6	5.7	11.2
Thiamin . . . . .mg	0.017	0.015	0.029
Riboflavin . . . . .mg	0.041	0.036	0.070
Niacin . . . . .mg	0.990	0.861	1.683
Pantothenic acid . . . . .mg	0.170	0.148	0.289
Vitamin B6 . . . . .mg	0.018	0.016	0.031
Folacin .mcg	3.4	3.0	5.8
Vitamin B12 . . . . .mcg	0	0	0
Vitamin A . . . . { RE	54	47	91
IU	535	465	910

PEARS, Raw

Nutrients and units	Amount in 100 grams, edible portion	Amount in edible portion of common measures of food	
	Mean	Approximate measure and weight 1 fruit = 166 g	1 c slices = 165 g
A	B	E	F
PROXIMATE:			
Water . . . . .g	83.81	139.13	138.29
Food energy { kcal	59	98	97
kj	247	410	408
Protein (N x 6.25) . . . . .g	0.39	0.65	0.65
Total lipid (fat) . . . . .g	0.40	0.66	0.66
Carbohydrate, total . . . . .g	15.11	25.09	24.94
Fiber . . . . .g	1.40	2.32	2.31
Ash . . . . .g	0.28	0.47	0.47
MINERALS:			
Calcium .mg	11	19	19
Iron . . . . .mg	0.25	0.41	0.41
Magnesium . . . . .mg	6	9	9
Phosphorus . . . . .mg	11	18	18
Potassium . . . . .mg	125	208	207
Sodium . . . . .mg	0	1	1
Zinc . . . . .mg	0.12	0.20	0.20
Copper . . . . .mg	0.113	0.188	0.186
Manganese . . . . .mg	0.076	0.126	0.125
VITAMINS:			
Ascorbic acid . . . . .mg	4.0	6.6	6.6
Thiamin . . . . .mg	0.020	0.033	0.033
Riboflavin . . . . .mg	0.040	0.066	0.066
Niacin . . . . .mg	0.100	0.166	0.165
Pantothenic acid . . . . .mg	0.070	0.116	0.116
Vitamin B6 . . . . .mg	0.018	0.030	0.030
Folacin .mcg	7.3	12.1	12.0
Vitamin B12 . . . . .mcg	0	0	0
Vitamin A . . . . { RE	2	3	3
IU	20	33	33

PEARS, Canned, water pack

Nutrients and units	Amount in 100 grams, edible portion	Amount in edible portion of common measures of food	
	Mean	Approximate measure and weight	
		1 half, 1⅔ tbsp liq. = 77 g	1 c halves = 244 g
——— A ———	—— B ——	—— E ——	—— F ——
PROXIMATE:			
Water . . . . .g	91.81	70.69	224.01
Food energy . . . . { kcal	29	22	71
{ kj	121	93	296
Protein (N x 6.25) . . . . .g	0.19	0.15	0.46
Total lipid (fat) . . . . .g	0.03	0.02	0.07
Carbohydrate, total . . . . .g	7.81	6.01	19.06
Fiber . . . . .g	0.61	0.47	1.49
Ash . . . . .g	0.16	0.13	0.40
MINERALS:			
Calcium .mg	4	3	9
Iron . . . . .mg	0.21	0.16	0.52
Magnesium . . . . .mg	4	3	9
Phosphorus . . . . .mg	7	5	17
Potassium . . . . .mg	53	41	130
Sodium .mg	2	2	5
Zinc . . . . .mg	0.09	0.07	0.21
Copper .mg	0.051	0.039	0.124
Manganese . . . . .mg	0.034	0.026	0.083
VITAMINS:			
Ascorbic acid . . . . .mg	1.0	0.8	2.5
Thiamin . . . . .mg	0.008	0.006	0.020
Riboflavin . . . . .mg	0.010	0.008	0.024
Niacin . . . . .mg	0.054	0.042	0.132
Pantothenic acid . . . . .mg	0.022	0.017	0.054
Vitamin B_6 . . . . .mg	0.014	0.011	0.034
Folacin .mcg	1.2	1.0	3.0
Vitamin B_{12} . . . . .mcg	0	0	0
Vitamin A . . . . { RE	0	0	0
{ IU	0	0	0

PINEAPPLE, Raw

Nutrients and units	Amount in 100 grams, edible portion	Amount in edible portion of common measures of food	
	Mean	Approximate measure and weight	
		1 slice = 84 g	1 c diced pieces = 155 g
——— A ———	—— B ——	—— E ——	—— F ——
PROXIMATE:			
Water . . . . .g	86.50	72.66	134.08
Food energy . . . . { kcal	49	42	77
{ kj	207	174	321
Protein (N x 6.25) . . . . .g	0.39	0.32	0.60
Total lipid (fat) . . . . .g	0.43	0.36	0.66
Carbohydrate, total . . . . .g	12.39	10.41	19.21
Fiber . . . . .g	0.54	0.45	0.84
Ash . . . . .g	0.29	0.25	0.45
MINERALS:			
Calcium .mg	7	6	11
Iron . . . . .mg	0.37	0.31	0.57
Magnesium . . . . .mg	14	11	21
Phosphorus . . . . .mg	7	6	11
Potassium . . . . .mg	113	95	175
Sodium .mg	1	1	1
Zinc . . . . .mg	0.08	0.07	0.12
Copper .mg	0.110	0.092	0.171
Manganese . . . . .mg	1.649	1.385	2.556
VITAMINS:			
Ascorbic acid . . . . .mg	15.4	13.0	23.9
Thiamin . . . . .mg	0.092	0.077	0.143
Riboflavin . . . . .mg	0.036	0.030	0.056
Niacin . . . . .mg	0.420	0.353	0.651
Pantothenic acid . . . . .mg	0.160	0.134	0.248
Vitamin B_6 . . . . .mg	0.087	0.073	0.135
Folacin .mcg	10.6	8.9	16.4
Vitamin B_{12} . . . . .mcg	0	0	0
Vitamin A . . . . { RE	2	2	4
{ IU	23	19	35

PINEAPPLE, Canned, water pack

Nutrients and units	Amount in 100 grams, edible portion	Amount in edible portion of common measures of food	
	Mean	Approximate measure and weight	
		1 slice, 1¼ tbsp liq. = 58 g	1 c tidbits = 246 g
A	B	E	F
PROXIMATE:			
Water . . . . g	90.82	52.68	223.42
Food energy . . . . { kcal	32	19	79
kj	134	78	330
Protein (N x 6.25) . . . . g	0.43	0.25	1.06
Total lipid (fat) . . . . g	0.09	0.05	0.23
Carbohydrate, total . . . . g	8.30	4.81	20.42
Fiber . . . . g	0.45	0.26	1.11
Ash . . . . g	0.35	0.21	0.87
MINERALS:			
Calcium . . . . mg	15	9	37
Iron . . . . mg	0.40	0.23	0.98
Magnesium . . . . mg	18	10	44
Phosphorus . . . . mg	4	2	10
Potassium . . . . mg	127	74	313
Sodium . . . . mg	1	1	3
Zinc . . . . mg	0.12	0.07	0.29
Copper . . . . mg	0.105	0.061	0.258
Manganese . . . . mg	1.121	0.650	2.758
VITAMINS:			
Ascorbic acid . . . . mg	7.7	4.5	18.9
Thiamin . . . . mg	0.093	0.054	0.229
Riboflavin . . . . mg	0.026	0.015	0.064
Niacin . . . . mg	0.298	0.173	0.733
Pantothenic acid . . . . mg	0.100	0.058	0.246
Vitamin B_6 . . . . mg	0.074	0.043	0.182
Folacin . . . . mcg	4.8	2.8	11.9
Vitamin B_{12} . . . . mcg	0	0	0
Vitamin A . . . . { RE	2	1	4
IU	15	9	37

PLUMS, Raw

Nutrients and units	Amount in 100 grams, edible portion	Amount in edible portion of common measures of food	
	Mean	Approximate measure and weight	
		1 fruit = 66 g	1 c slices = 165 g
A	B	E	F
PROXIMATE:			
Water . . . . g	85.20	56.23	140.57
Food energy . . . . { kcal	55	36	91
kj	230	152	380
Protein (N x 6.25) . . . . g	0.79	0.52	1.30
Total lipid (fat) . . . . g	0.62	0.41	1.02
Carbohydrate, total . . . . g	13.01	8.59	21.47
Fiber . . . . g	0.60	0.40	0.99
Ash . . . . g	0.39	0.26	0.65
MINERALS:			
Calcium . . . . mg	4	2	6
Iron . . . . mg	0.10	0.07	0.17
Magnesium . . . . mg	7	4	11
Phosphorus . . . . mg	10	7	17
Potassium . . . . mg	172	113	284
Sodium . . . . mg	0	0	1
Zinc . . . . mg	0.10	0.06	0.16
Copper . . . . mg	0.043	0.028	0.071
Manganese . . . . mg	0.049	0.032	0.081
VITAMINS:			
Ascorbic acid . . . . mg	9.5	6.3	15.8
Thiamin . . . . mg	0.043	0.028	0.071
Riboflavin . . . . mg	0.096	0.063	0.158
Niacin . . . . mg	0.500	0.330	0.825
Pantothenic acid . . . . mg	0.182	0.120	0.300
Vitamin B_6 . . . . mg	0.081	0.053	0.134
Folacin . . . . mcg	2.2	1.4	3.6
Vitamin B_{12} . . . . mcg	0	0	0
Vitamin A . . . . { RE	32	21	53
IU	323	213	533

RAISINS, Seedless

Nutrients and units	Amount in 100 grams, edible portion	Amount in edible portion of common measures of food	
	Mean	Approximate measure and weight	
		1 c not packed = 145 g	1 c packed = 165 g
A	B	E	F
PROXIMATE:			
Water . . . . .g	15.42	22.36	25.44
Food energy { kcal	300	434	494
{ kj	1,253	1,817	2,068
Protein (N x 6.25) . . . . .g	3.22	4.67	5.32
Total lipid (fat) . . . . .g	0.46	0.67	0.76
Carbohydrate, total . . . . .g	79.13	114.73	130.56
Fiber . . . . .g	1.28	1.85	2.11
Ash . . . . .g	1.77	2.57	2.92
MINERALS:			
Calcium . . . . .mg	49	71	81
Iron . . . . .mg	2.08	3.02	3.43
Magnesium . . . . .mg	33	48	54
Phosphorus . . . . .mg	97	140	159
Potassium . . . . .mg	751	1,089	1,239
Sodium .mg	12	17	19
Zinc . . . . .mg	0.27	0.38	0.44
Copper .mg	0.309	0.448	0.510
Manganese . . . . .mg	0.308	0.447	0.508
VITAMINS:			
Ascorbic acid . . . . .mg	3.3	4.8	5.5
Thiamin . . . . .mg	0.156	0.226	0.257
Riboflavin . . . . .mg	0.088	0.128	0.145
Niacin . . . . .mg	0.818	1.186	1.350
Pantothenic acid . . . . .mg	0.045	0.065	0.074
Vitamin B_6 . . . . .mg	0.249	0.361	0.411
Folacin . . . . .mcg	3.3	4.8	5.5
Vitamin B_{12} . . . . .mcg	0	0	0
Vitamin A . . . . { RE	1	1	1
{ IU	8	11	13

RASPBERRIES, Raw

Nutrients and units	Amount in 100 grams, edible portion	Amount in edible portion of common measures of food	
	Mean	Approximate measure and weight	
		1 c = 123 g	1 pint = 312 g
A	B	E	F
PROXIMATE:			
Water . . . . .g	86.57	106.48	270.09
Food energy { kcal	49	61	154
{ kj	206	254	644
Protein (N x 6.25) . . . . .g	0.91	1.11	2.83
Total lipid (fat) . . . . .g	0.55	0.68	1.72
Carbohydrate, total . . . . .g	11.57	14.24	36.11
Fiber . . . . .g	3.00	3.69	9.36
Ash . . . . .g	0.40	0.50	1.26
MINERALS:			
Calcium . . . . .mg	22	27	69
Iron . . . . .mg	0.57	0.70	1.78
Magnesium . . . . .mg	18	22	55
Phosphorus . . . . .mg	12	15	37
Potassium . . . . .mg	152	187	474
Sodium .mg	0	0	0
Zinc . . . . .mg	0.46	0.57	1.44
Copper .mg	0.074	0.091	0.231
Manganese . . . . .mg	1.013	1.246	3.161
VITAMINS:			
Ascorbic acid . . . . .mg	25.0	30.8	78.0
Thiamin . . . . .mg	0.030	0.037	0.094
Riboflavin . . . . .mg	0.090	0.111	0.281
Niacin . . . . .mg	0.900	1.107	2.808
Pantothenic acid . . . . .mg	0.240	0.295	0.749
Vitamin B_6 . . . . .mg	0.057	0.070	0.178
Folacin . . . . .mcg			
Vitamin B_{12} . . . . .mcg	0	0	0
Vitamin A . . . . { RE	13	16	41
{ IU	130	160	406

STRAWBERRIES, Raw

Nutrients and units	Amount in 100 grams, edible portion	Amount in edible portion of common measures of food	
	Mean	Approximate measure and weight 1 c = 149 g	1 pint = 320 g
A	B	E	F
PROXIMATE:			
Water ....g	91.57	136.44	293.02
Food energy .... { kcal	30	45	97
{ kj	127	190	407
Protein (N x 6.25) ....g	0.61	0.91	1.96
Total lipid (fat) ....g	0.37	0.55	1.18
Carbohydrate, total ....g	7.02	10.47	22.48
Fiber ....g	0.53	0.79	1.70
Ash ....g	0.43	0.63	1.36
MINERALS:			
Calcium ....mg	14	21	45
Iron ....mg	0.38	0.57	1.23
Magnesium ....mg	10	16	34
Phosphorus ....mg	19	28	60
Potassium ....mg	166	247	530
Sodium ....mg	1	2	4
Zinc ....mg	0.13	0.19	0.40
Copper ....mg	0.049	0.073	0.157
Manganese ....mg	0.290	0.432	0.928
VITAMINS:			
Ascorbic acid..............mg	56.7	84.5	181.5
Thiamin ....mg	0.020	0.030	0.064
Riboflavin ....mg	0.066	0.098	0.211
Niacin....................mg	0.230	0.343	0.736
Pantothenic acid ....mg	0.340	0.507	1.088
Vitamin B_6...............mg	0.059	0.088	0.189
Folacin ....mcg	17.7	26.4	56.6
Vitamin B_{12} ....mcg	0	0	0
Vitamin A............. { RE	3	4	9
{ IU	27	41	87

TANGERINE JUICE, Raw

Nutrients and units	Amount in 100 grams, edible portion	Amount in edible portion of common measures of food	
	Mean	Approximate measure and weight 1 fl oz = 30.9 g	1 c = 247 g
A	B	E	F
PROXIMATE:			
Water ....g	88.90	27.47	219.58
Food energy .... { kcal	43	13	106
{ hj	180	56	444
Protein (N x 6.25) ....g	0.50	0.15	1.24
Total lipid (fat) ....g	0.20	0.06	0.49
Carbohydrate, total ....g	10.10	3.12	24.95
Fiber ....g	0.10	0.03	0.25
Ash ....g	0.30	0.09	0.74
MINERALS:			
Calcium ....mg	18	6	44
Iron ....mg	0.20	0.06	0.49
Magnesium ....mg	8	2	20
Phosphorus................mg	14	4	35
Potassium ....mg	178	55	440
Sodium ....mg	1	0	2
Zinc ....mg	0.03	0.01	0.06
Copper ....mg	0.025	0.008	0.062
Manganese ....mg	0.037	0.011	0.091
VITAMINS:			
Ascorbic acid..............mg	31.0	9.6	76.6
Thiamin ....mg	0.060	0.019	0.148
Riboflavin ....mg	0.020	0.006	0.049
Niacin....................mg	0.100	0.031	0.247
Pantothenic acid ....mg			
Vitamin B_6...............mg			
Folacin ....mcg			
Vitamin B_{12} ....mcg	0	0	0
Vitamin A............. { RE	42	13	104
{ IU	420	130	1,037

WATERMELON, Raw

Nutrients and units		Amount in 100 grams, edible portion	Amount in edible portion of common measures of food	
		Mean	Approximate measure and weight	
			1/16 fruit = 482 g	1 c diced pieces = 160 g
A		B	E	F
PROXIMATE:				
Water	g	91.51	441.08	146.42
Food energy	kcal	32	152	50
	kj	132	635	211
Protein (N x 6.25)	g	0.62	2.97	0.99
Total lipid (fat)	g	0.43	2.06	0.68
Carbohydrate, total	g	7.18	34.62	11.49
Fiber	g	0.30	1.45	0.48
Ash	g	0.26	1.27	0.42
MINERALS:				
Calcium	mg	8	38	13
Iron	mg	0.17	0.83	0.28
Magnesium	mg	11	52	17
Phosphorus	mg	9	41	14
Potassium	mg	116	560	186
Sodium	mg	2	10	3
Zinc	mg	0.07	0.34	0.11
Copper	mg	0.032	0.154	0.051
Manganese	mg	0.037	0.178	0.059
VITAMINS:				
Ascorbic acid	mg	9.6	46.5	15.4
Thiamin	mg	0.080	0.386	0.128
Riboflavin	mg	0.020	0.096	0.032
Niacin	mg	0.200	0.964	0.320
Pantothenic acid	mg	0.212	1.022	0.339
Vitamin B$_6$	mg	0.144	0.694	0.230
Folacin	mcg	2.2	10.4	3.4
Vitamin B$_{12}$	mcg	0	0	0
Vitamin A	RE	37	176	58
	IU	366	762	585

ASPARAGUS, Cooked, boiled, drained

Nutrients and units	Amount in 100 grams, edible portion	Amount in edible portion of common measures of food	
	Mean	Approximate measure and weight	
		½ c = 90 g	4 spears = 60 g
A	B	E	F
PROXIMATE:			
Water . . . . .g	92.04	82.84	55.23
Food energy . . . . { kcal	25	22	15
{ kj	103	93	62
Protein (N x 6.25) . . . . .g	2.59	2.33	1.55
Total lipid (fat) . . . . .g	0.31	0.28	0.19
Carbohydrate, total . . . . .g	4.40	3.96	2.64
Fiber . . . . .g	0.83	0.75	0.50
Ash . . . . .g	0.66	0.59	0.40
MINERALS:			
Calcium . . . . .mg	24	22	15
Iron . . . . .mg	0.66	0.59	0.40
Magnesium . . . . .mg	19	17	11
Phosphorus . . . . .mg	61	54	36
Potassium . . . . .mg	310	279	186
Sodium . . . . .mg	4	4	3
Zinc . . . . .mg	0.48	0.43	0.29
Copper .mg	0.100	0.090	0.060
Manganese . . . . .mg	0.208	0.187	0.125
VITAMINS:			
Ascorbic acid . . . . .mg	27.1	18.2	15.7
Thiamin . . . . .mg	0.099	0.089	0.059
Riboflavin . . . . .mg	0.121	0.109	0.073
Niacin . . . . .mg	1.052	0.947	0.631
Pantothenic acid . . . . .mg	0.161	0.145	0.097
Vitamin B₆ . . . . .mg	0.141	0.127	0.085
Folacin . . . . .mcg	98.1	88.2	58.8
Vitamin B₁₂ . . . . .mcg	0	0	0
Vitamin A . . . . { RE	83	75	50
{ IU	829	746	498

ASPARAGUS, Canned, solids and liquid

Nutrients and units	Amount in 100 grams, edible portion	Amount in edible portion of common measures of food	
	Mean	Approximate measure and weight	
		½ c = 122 g	1 can = 411 g
A	B	E	F
PROXIMATE:			
Water . . . . g	94.63	115.44	388.91
Food energy { kcal	14	17	58
{ kj	59	72	242
Protein (N x 6.25) . . . . g	1.80	2.20	7.41
Total lipid (fat) . . . . g	0.19	0.23	0.79
Carbohydrate, total . . . . g	2.25	2.75	9.26
Fiber . . . . g	0.53	0.64	2.17
Ash . . . . g	1.13	1.37	4.63
MINERALS:			
Calcium . . . . mg	14	17	58
Iron . . . . mg	0.58	0.71	2.38
Magnesium . . . . mg	9	11	38
Phosphorus . . . . mg	38	46	156
Potassium . . . . mg	153	186	628
Sodium . . . . mg	348	425	1,432
Zinc . . . . mg	0.47	0.57	1.92
Copper . . . . mg	0.107	0.131	0.440
Manganese . . . . mg	0.152	0.185	0.625
VITAMINS:			
Ascorbic acid . . . . mg	16.4	20.0	67.4
Thiamin . . . . mg	0.054	0.066	0.222
Riboflavin . . . . mg	0.089	0.109	0.366
Niacin . . . . mg	0.851	1.038	3.498
Pantothenic acid . . . . mg	0.124	0.151	0.510
Vitamin B$_6$ . . . . mg	0.098	0.120	0.403
Folacin . . . . mcg	85.3	104.1	350.6
Vitamin B$_{12}$ . . . . mcg	0	0	0
Vitamin A . . . . { RE	47	58	195
{ IU	474	578	1,948

BEANS, LIMA, (Fordhook), Frozen, cooked, boiled, drained

Nutrients and units	Amount in 100 grams, edible portion	Amount in edible portion of common measures of food	
	Mean	Approximate measure and weight	
		Yield, 10 oz pkg = 311 g	½ c = 85 g
A	B	E	F
PROXIMATE:			
Water . . . . g	73.50	228.59	62.48
Food energy { kcal	100	312	85
{ kj	420	1,306	357
Protein (N x 6.25) . . . . g	6.07	18.87	5.16
Total lipid (fat) . . . . g	0.34	1.04	0.29
Carbohydrate, total . . . . g	18.80	58.46	15.98
Fiber . . . . g	1.87	5.82	1.59
Ash . . . . g	1.30	4.05	1.10
MINERALS:			
Calcium . . . . mg	22	67	19
Iron . . . . mg	1.36	4.23	1.16
Magnesium . . . . mg	34	107	29
Phosphorus . . . . mg	63	197	54
Potassium . . . . mg	408	1,268	347
Sodium . . . . mg	53	164	45
Zinc . . . . mg	0.44	1.37	0.37
Copper . . . . mg	0.055	0.171	0.047
Manganese . . . . mg	0.311	0.967	0.264
VITAMINS:			
Ascorbic acid . . . . mg	12.8	39.9	10.9
Thiamin . . . . mg	0.074	0.230	0.063
Riboflavin . . . . mg	0.061	0.190	0.052
Niacin . . . . mg	1.069	3.325	0.909
Pantothenic acid . . . . mg	0.163	0.507	0.139
Vitamin B$_6$ . . . . mg	0.122	0.379	0.104
Folacin . . . . mcg			
Vitamin B$_{12}$ . . . . mcg	0	0	0
Vitamin A . . . . { RE	19	59	16
{ IU	190	592	162

BEANS, MUNG, Mature seeds, sprouted, raw

Nutrients and units		Amount in 100 grams, edible portion	Amount in edible portion of common measures of food	
		Mean	Approximate measure and weight	
			½ c = 52 g	12 oz pkg = 340 g
A		B	E	F
PROXIMATE:				
Water .... g		90.40	47.01	307.37
Food energy .... {	kcal	30	16	102
	kj	126	65	427
Protein (N x 6.25) .... g		3.04	1.58	10.34
Total lipid (fat) .... g		0.18	0.10	0.63
Carbohydrate, total .... g		5.93	3.08	20.17
Fiber .... g		0.81	0.42	2.77
Ash .... g		0.44	0.23	1.50
MINERALS:				
Calcium .... mg		13	7	43
Iron .... mg		0.91	0.47	3.08
Magnesium .... mg		21	11	72
Phosphorus.................. mg		54	28	184
Potassium .... mg		149	77	505
Sodium .... mg		6	3	19
Zinc .... mg		0.41	0.21	1.39
Copper .... mg		0.164	0.085	0.558
Manganese .... mg		0.188	0.098	0.639
VITAMINS:				
Ascorbic acid................. mg		13.2	6.8	44.7
Thiamin .... mg		0.084	0.044	0.286
Riboflavin .... mg		0.124	0.064	0.422
Niacin .... mg		0.749	0.389	2.547
Pantothenic acid .... mg		0.380	0.198	1.292
Vitamin B_6 .... mg		0.088	0.046	0.299
Folacin .... mcg		60.8	31.6	206.7
Vitamin B_{12} .... mcg		0	0	0
Vitamin A................. {	RE	2	1	7
	IU	21	11	71

BEANS, SNAP, Frozen, cooked, boiled, drained

Includes Italian, green, and yellow varieties.

Nutrients and units		Amount in 100 grams, edible portion	Amount in edible portion of common measures of food	
		Mean	Approximate measure and weight	
			½ c = 68 g	1 c = 135 g
A		B	E	F
PROXIMATE:				
Water .... g		91.94	62.52	124.11
Food energy .... {	kcal	26	18	36
	kj	110	75	149
Protein (N x 6.25) .... g		1.36	0.92	1.84
Total lipid (fat) .... g		0.14	0.09	0.18
Carbohydrate, total .... g		6.12	4.16	8.26
Fiber .... g		1.03	0.70	1.39
Ash .... g		0.45	0.30	0.60
MINERALS:				
Calcium .... mg		45	31	61
Iron .... mg		0.82	0.56	1.11
Magnesium .... mg		21	15	29
Phosphorus .... mg		24	16	33
Potassium .... mg		112	76	151
Sodium .... mg		13	9	17
Zinc .... mg		0.62	0.42	0.84
Copper .... mg		0.067	0.046	0.090
Manganese .... mg		0.371	0.252	0.501
VITAMINS:				
Ascorbic acid................. mg		8.2	5.6	11.1
Thiamin .... mg		0.048	0.033	0.065
Riboflavin .... mg		0.074	0.050	0.100
Niacin .... mg		0.417	0.284	0.563
Pantothenic acid .... mg		0.055	0.037	0.074
Vitamin B_6 .... mg		0.056	0.038	0.076
Folacin .... mcg				
Vitamin B_{12} .... mcg		0	0	0
Vitamin A................. {	RE	53	36	71
	IU	528	359	713

BEETS, Raw

Nutrients and units	Amount in 100 grams, edible portion	Amount in edible portion of common measures of food	
	Mean	Approximate measure and weight	
		½ c slices = 68 g	2 beets = 163 g
A	B	E	F
PROXIMATE:			
Water .... g	87.32	59.38	142.33
Food energy .... { kcal	44	30	71
{ kj	183	124	298
Protein (N x 6.25) .... g	1.48	1.01	2.41
Total lipid (fat) .... g	0.14	0.10	0.23
Carbohydrate, total .... g	10.00	6.80	16.30
Fiber .... g	0.80	0.54	1.30
Ash .... g	1.06	0.72	1.73
MINERALS:			
Calcium .... mg	16	11	25
Iron .... mg	0.91	0.62	1.49
Magnesium .... mg	21	14	34
Phosphorus .... mg	48	33	78
Potassium .... mg	324	220	528
Sodium .... mg	72	49	118
Zinc .... mg	0.37	0.25	0.60
Copper .... mg	0.083	0.056	0.135
Manganese .... mg	0.352	0.239	0.574
VITAMINS:			
Ascorbic acid................. mg	11.0	7.5	17.9
Thiamin .... mg	0.050	0.034	0.082
Riboflavin .... mg	0.020	0.014	0.033
Niacin .... mg	0.400	0.272	0.652
Pantothenic acid .... mg	0.150	0.102	0.245
Vitamin B$_6$ .... mg	0.046	0.031	0.075
Folacin .... mcg	92.6	63.0	150.9
Vitamin B$_{12}$ .... mcg	0	0	0
Vitamin A................. { RE	2	1	3
{ IU	20	14	33

BROCCOLI, Cooked, boiled, drained

Nutrients and units	Amount in 100 grams, edible portion	Amount in edible portion of common measures of food	
	Mean	Approximate measure and weight	
		½ c chopped = 78 g	1 spear = 180 g
A	B	E	F
PROXIMATE:			
Water .... g	90.20	70.36	162.36
Food energy .... { kcal	29	23	53
{ kj	123	96	222
Protein (N x 6.25) .... g	2.97	2.32	5.35
Total lipid (fat) .... g	0.28	0.22	0.50
Carbohydrate, total .... g	5.57	4.34	10.02
Fiber .... g	1.20	0.94	2.16
Ash .... g	0.99	0.77	1.77
MINERALS:			
Calcium .... mg	114	89	205
Iron .... mg	1.15	0.89	2.06
Magnesium .... mg	60	47	108
Phosphorus .... mg	48	37	86
Potassium .... mg	163	127	293
Sodium .... mg	11	8	19
Zinc .... mg	0.15	0.12	0.27
Copper .... mg	0.069	0.054	0.124
Manganese .... mg	0.245	0.191	0.441
VITAMINS:			
Ascorbic acid................. mg	62.8	49.0	113.0
Thiamin .... mg	0.082	0.064	0.148
Riboflavin .... mg	0.207	0.161	0.373
Niacin .... mg	0.755	0.589	1.359
Pantothenic acid .... mg	0.288	0.225	0.518
Vitamin B$_6$ .... mg	0.198	0.154	0.356
Folacin .... mcg	68.4	53.3	123.1
Vitamin B$_{12}$ .... mcg	0	0	0
Vitamin A................. { RE	141	110	254
{ IU	1,409	1,099	2,537

BROCCOLI, Frozen, chopped, unprepared

Nutrients and units		Amount in 100 grams, edible portion	Amount in edible portion of common measures of food	
		Mean	Approximate measure and weight	
			10 oz pkg = 284 g	2 lb pkg = 907 g
A		B	E	F
PROXIMATE:				
Water	g	91.46	259.74	829.52
Food energy	kcal	26	75	239
	kj	110	313	999
Protein (N x 6.25)	g	2.81	7.97	25.46
Total lipid (fat)	g	0.29	0.81	2.59
Carbohydrate, total	g	4.79	13.59	43.40
Fiber	g	1.10	3.13	9.99
Ash	g	0.66	1.89	6.02
MINERALS:				
Calcium	mg	56	159	507
Iron	mg	0.81	2.30	7.34
Magnesium	mg	18	50	160
Phosphorus	mg	50	142	454
Potassium	mg	212	602	1,922
Sodium	mg	24	68	216
Zinc	mg	0.48	1.37	4.39
Copper	mg	0.038	0.108	0.345
Manganese	mg	0.294	0.835	2.667
VITAMINS:				
Ascorbic acid	mg	56.4	160.2	511.5
Thiamin	mg	0.053	0.151	0.481
Riboflavin	mg	0.096	0.273	0.871
Niacin	mg	0.470	1.335	4 263
Pantothenic acid	mg	0.279	0.792	2.531
Vitamin B_6	mg	0.130	0.369	1.179
Folacin	mcg	67.0	190.2	607.4
Vitamin B_{12}	mcg	0	0	0
Vitamin A	RE	207	587	1,873
	IU	2,066	5,866	18,735

BRUSSELS SPROUTS, Cooked, boiled, drained

Nutrients and units		Amount in 100 grams, edible portion	Amount in edible portion of common measures of food	
		Mean	Approximate measure and weight	
			1 sprout = 21 g	½ c = 78 g
A		B	E	F
PROXIMATE:				
Water	g	87.32	18.34	68.11
Food energy	kcal	39	8	30
	kj	162	34	126
Protein (N x 6.25)	g	2.55	0.53	1.99
Total lipid (fat)	g	0.51	0.11	0.40
Carbohydrate, total	g	8.67	1.82	6.76
Fiber	g	1.37	0.29	1.07
Ash	g	0.95	0.20	0.74
MINERALS:				
Calcium	mg	36	7	28
Iron	mg	1.20	0.25	0.94
Magnesium	mg	20	4	16
Phosphorus	mg	56	12	44
Potassium	mg	317	67	247
Sodium	mg	21	4	17
Zinc	mg	0.33	0.07	0.25
Copper	mg	0.083	0.017	0.065
Manganese	mg	0.227	0.048	0.177
VITAMINS:				
Ascorbic acid	mg	62.0	13.0	48.4
Thiamin	mg	0.107	0.022	0.083
Riboflavin	mg	0.080	0.017	0.062
Niacin	mg	0.607	0.127	0.473
Pantothenic acid	mg	0.252	0.053	0.197
Vitamin B_6	mg	0.178	0.037	0.139
Folacin	mcg	60.0	12.6	46.8
Vitamin B_{12}	mcg	0	0	0
Vitamin A	RE	72	15	56
	IU	719	151	561

BRUSSELS SPROUTS, Frozen, unprepared

Nutrients and units		Amount in 100 grams, edible portion	Amount in edible portion of common measures of food	
		Mean	Approximate measure and weight	
			10 oz pkg = 284 g	2 lb pkg = 907 g
A		B	E	F
PROXIMATE:				
Water ....g		87.07	247.27	789.69
Food energy	kcal	41	116	369
	kj	170	484	1,545
Protein (N x 6.25) ....g		3.78	10.72	34.24
Total lipid (fat) ....g		0.41	1.16	3.69
Carbohydrate, total ....g		7.87	22.36	71.40
Fiber ....g		1.41	4.01	12.80
Ash ....g		0.88	2.50	7.98
MINERALS:				
Calcium ....mg		26	75	239
Iron ....mg		0.93	2.65	8.46
Magnesium ....mg		20	57	182
Phosphorus................mg		62	176	563
Potassium ....mg		370	1,052	3,359
Sodium ....mg		10	28	89
Zinc ....mg		0.31	0.87	2.78
Copper ....mg		0.033	0.094	0.299
Manganese ....mg		0.311	0.883	2.821
VITAMINS:				
Ascorbic acid................mg		74.1	210.4	672.0
Thiamin ....mg		0.105	0.298	0.952
Riboflavin ....mg		0.122	0.346	1.107
Niacin.....................mg		0.638	1.812	5.787
Pantothenic acid ....mg		0.285	0.809	2.585
Vitamin B_6..................mg		0.202	0.574	1.832
Folacin ....mcg		123.4	350.6	1,119.6
Vitamin B_{12} ....mcg		0	0	0
Vitamin A.................	RE	81	231	739
	IU	815	2,314	7,389

CABBAGE, Raw

Includes Danish, domestic, and pointed types.

Nutrients and units		Amount in 100 grams, edible portion	Amount in edible portion of common measures of food	
		Mean	Approximate measure and weight	
			½ c shredded = 35 g	1 head = 908 g
A		B	E	F
PROXIMATE:				
Water ....g		92.52	32.38	840.06
Food energy	kcal	24	8	215
	kj	99	35	898
Protein (N x 6.25) ....g		1.21	0.42	11.00
Total lipid (fat) ....g		0.18	0.06	1.63
Carbohydrate, total ....g		5.37	1.88	48.78
Fiber ....g		0.80	0.28	7.26
Ash ....g		0.72	0.25	6.53
MINERALS:				
Calcium ....mg		47	16	424
Iron ....mg		0.56	0.20	5.09
Magnesium ....mg		15	5	134
Phosphorus................mg		23	8	211
Potassium ....mg		246	86	2,231
Sodium ....mg		18	6	164
Zinc ....mg		0.18	0.06	1.66
Copper ....mg		0.023	0.008	0.209
Manganese ....mg		0.159	0.056	1.444
VITAMINS:				
Ascorbic acid................mg		47.3	16.5	429.2
Thiamin ....mg		0.050	0.018	0.454
Riboflavin ....mg		0.030	0.011	0.272
Niacin.....................mg		0.300	0.105	2.724
Pantothenic acid ....mg		0.140	0.049	1.271
Vitamin B_6..................mg		0.095	0.033	0.863
Folacin ....mcg		56.7	19.8	514.8
Vitamin B_{12} ....mcg		0	0	0
Vitamin A.................	RE	13	4	114
	IU	126	44	1,143

CABBAGE, Cooked, boiled, drained

Includes Danish, domestic, and pointed types.

Nutrients and units	Amount in 100 grams, edible portion	Amount in edible portion of common measures of food	
	Mean	Approximate measure and weight	
		½ c shredded = 75 g	1 head = 1,262 g
A	B	E	F
PROXIMATE:			
Water ....g	93.60	70.20	1,181.19
Food energy { kcal	21	16	270
{ kj	90	67	1,130
Protein (N x 6.25) ....g	0.96	0.72	12.08
Total lipid (fat) ....g	0.25	0.18	3.10
Carbohydrate, total ....g	4.77	3.57	60.15
Fiber ....g	0.60	0.45	7.57
Ash ....g	0.43	0.33	5.48
MINERALS:			
Calcium ....mg	33	25	413
Iron ....mg	0.39	0.29	4.96
Magnesium ....mg	15	11	184
Phosphorus..................mg	25	18	309
Potassium ....mg	205	154	2,593
Sodium ....mg	19	14	239
Zinc ....mg	0.16	0.12	1.96
Copper ....mg	0.028	0.021	0.353
Manganese ....mg	0.129	0.097	1.628
VITAMINS:			
Ascorbic acid.................mg	24.3	18.2	306.7
Thiamin ....mg	0.057	0.043	0.719
Riboflavin ....mg	0.055	0.041	0.694
Niacin......................mg	0.230	0.173	2.903
Pantothenic acid ....mg	0.063	0.047	0.795
Vitamin B_6 ....mg	0.064	0.048	0.808
Folacin ....mcg	20.3	15.2	255.6
Vitamin B_{12} ....mcg	0	0	0
Vitamin A................ { RE	9	6	108
{ IU	86	64	1,079

CARROTS, Raw

Nutrients and units	Amount in 100 grams, edible portion	Amount in edible portion of common measures of food	
	Mean	Approximate measure and weight	
		½ c shredded = 55 g	1 carrot = 72 g
A	B	E	F
PROXIMATE:			
Water ....g	87.79	48.29	63.21
Food energy { kcal	43	24	31
{ kj	181	99	130
Protein (N x 6.25) ....g	1.03	0.56	0.74
Total lipid (fat) ....g	0.19	0.10	0.14
Carbohydrate, total ....g	10.14	5.58	7.30
Fiber ....g	1.04	0.57	0.75
Ash ....g	0.87	0.48	0.63
MINERALS:			
Calcium ....mg	27	15	19
Iron ....mg	0.50	0.27	0.36
Magnesium ....mg	15	8	11
Phosphorus..................mg	44	24	32
Potassium ....mg	323	178	233
Sodium ....mg	35	19	25
Zinc ....mg	0.20	0.11	0.14
Copper ....mg	0.047	0.026	0.034
Manganese ....mg	0.142	0.078	0.102
VITAMINS:			
Ascorbic acid.................mg	9.3	5.1	6.7
Thiamin ....mg	0.097	0.053	0.070
Riboflavin ....mg	0.059	0.032	0.042
Niacin......................mg	0.928	0.510	0.668
Pantothenic acid ....mg	0.197	0.108	0.142
Vitamin B_6 ....mg	0.147	0.081	0.106
Folacin ....mcg	14.0	7.7	10.1
Vitamin B_{12} ....mcg	0	0	0
Vitamin A................ { RE	2,813	1,547	2,025
{ IU	28,129	15,471	20,253

CARROTS, Cooked, boiled, drained

Nutrients and units	Amount in 100 grams, edible portion	Amount in edible portion of common measures of food	
	Mean	Approximate measure and weight ½ c slices = 78 g	1 carrot = 46 g
A	B	E	F
PROXIMATE:			
Water . . . . .g	87.38	68.15	40.19
Food energy . . . . { kcal	45	35	21
{ kj	188	146	86
Protein (N x 6.25) . . . . .g	1.09	0.85	0.50
Total lipid (fat) . . . . .g	0.18	0.14	0.08
Carbohydrate, total . . . . .g	10.48	8.18	4.82
Fiber . . . . .g	1.47	1.15	0.68
Ash . . . . .g	0.87	0.68	0.40
MINERALS:			
Calcium . . . . .mg	31	24	14
Iron . . . . .mg	0.62	0.48	0.28
Magnesium . . . . .mg	13	10	6
Phosphorus . . . . .mg	30	24	14
Potassium . . . . .mg	227	177	104
Sodium .mg	66	52	30
Zinc . . . . .mg	0.30	0.23	0.14
Copper .mg	0.134	0.105	0.062
Manganese . . . . .mg	0.752	0.587	0.346
VITAMINS:			
Ascorbic acid . . . . .mg	2.3	1.8	1.1
Thiamin .mg	0.034	0.027	0.016
Riboflavin . . . . .mg	0.056	0.044	0.026
Niacin . . . . .mg	0.506	0.395	0.233
Pantothenic acid . . . . .mg	0.304	0.237	0.140
Vitamin B_6 . . . . .mg	0.246	0.192	0.113
Folacin .mcg	13.9	10.8	6.4
Vitamin B_{12} . . . . .mcg	0	0	0
Vitamin A . . . . { RE	2.455	1,915	1,129
{ IU	24,554	19,152	11,295

CARROT JUICE, Canned

Nutrients and units	Amount in 100 grams, edible portion	Amount in edible portion of common measures of food	
	Mean	Approximate measure and weight ½ c = 123 g	6 fl oz = 184 g
A	B	E	F
PROXIMATE:			
Water . . . . .g	88.87	109.31	163.52
Food energy . . . . { kcal	40	49	73
{ kj	165	203	304
Protein (N x 6.25) . . . . .g	0.95	1.17	1.74
Total lipid (fat) . . . . .g	0.15	0.18	0.27
Carbohydrate, total . . . . .g	9.29	11.42	17.09
Fiber . . . . .g	0.95	1.17	1.75
Ash . . . . .g	0.75	0.92	1.38
MINERALS:			
Calcium . . . . .mg	24	29	44
Iron . . . . .mg	0.46	0.57	0.85
Magnesium . . . . .mg	14	17	26
Phosphorus . . . . .mg	42	51	77
Potassium . . . . .mg	292	360	538
Sodium .mg	29	36	54
Zinc . . . . .mg	0.18	0.22	0.33
Copper .mg	0.046	0.057	0.085
Manganese . . . . .mg	0.130	0.160	0.239
VITAMINS:			
Ascorbic acid . . . . .mg	8.5	10.5	15.7
Thiamin .mg	0.092	0.113	0.169
Riboflavin . . . . .mg	0.055	0.068	0.101
Niacin . . . . .mg	0.386	0.475	0.710
Pantothenic acid . . . . .mg	0.228	0.280	0.420
Vitamin B_6 . . . . .mg	0.217	0.267	0.399
Folacin .mcg	3.8	4.7	7.0
Vitamin B_{12} . . . . .mcg	0	0	0
Vitamin A . . . . { RE	2,575	3,167	4.738
{ IU	25,751	31,673	47,381

CAULIFLOWER, Raw

Nutrients and units	Amount in 100 grams, edible portion	Amount in edible portion of common measures of food	
	Mean	Approximate measure and weight	
		½ c, 1 in pieces = 50 g	3 flowerets = 56 g
A	B	E	F
PROXIMATE:			
Water . . . . .g	92.26	46.13	51.66
Food energy . . . . { kcal	24	12	13
{ kj	100	50	56
Protein (N x 6.25) . . . . .g	1.99	0.99	1.11
Total lipid (fat) . . . . .g	0.18	0.09	0.10
Carbohydrate, total . . . . .g	4.92	2.46	2.76
Fiber . . . . .g	0.85	0.42	0.47
Ash . . . . .g	0.66	0.33	0.37
MINERALS:			
Calcium .mg	29	14	16
Iron . . . . .mg	0.58	0.29	0.32
Magnesium . . . . .mg	14	7	8
Phosphorus . . . . .mg	46	23	26
Potassium . . . . .mg	355	178	199
Sodium . . . . .mg	15	7	8
Zinc . . . . .mg	0.18	0.09	0.10
Copper .mg	0.032	0.016	0.018
Manganese . . . . .mg	0.203	0.102	0.114
VITAMINS:			
Ascorbic acid . . . . .mg	71.5	35.8	40.0
Thiamin . . . . .mg	0.076	0.038	0.043
Riboflavin . . . . .mg	0.057	0.029	0.032
Niacin . . . . .mg	0.633	0.317	0.354
Pantothenic acid . . . . .mg	0.141	0.071	0.079
Vitamin B_6 . . . . .mg	0.231	0.116	0.129
Folacin .mcg	66.1	33.1	37.0
Vitamin B_{12} . . . . .mcg	0	0	0
Vitamin A . . . . { RE	2	1	1
{ IU	16	8	9

CAULIFLOWER, Cooked, boiled, drained

Nutrients and units	Amount in 100 grams, edible portion	Amount in edible portion of common measures of food	
	Mean	Approximate measure and weight	
		½ c 1 in pieces = 62 g	3 flowerets = 54 g
A	B	E	F
PROXIMATE:			
Water . . . . .g	92.50	57.35	49.95
Food energy . . . . { kcal	24	15	13
{ kj	102	63	55
Protein (N x 6.25) . . . . .g	1.87	1.16	1.01
Total lipid (fat) . . . . .g	0.17	0.11	0.09
Carbohydrate, total . . . . .g	4.62	2.87	2.50
Fiber . . . . .g	0.82	0.51	0.44
Ash . . . . .g	0.62	0.38	0.33
MINERALS:			
Calcium .mg	27	17	14
Iron . . . . .mg	0.42	0.26	0.23
Magnesium . . . . .mg	11	7	6
Phosphorus . . . . .mg	35	22	19
Potassium . . . . .mg	323	200	174
Sodium . . . . .mg	6	4	3
Zinc . . . . .mg	0.24	0.15	0.13
Copper .mg	0.091	0.056	0.049
Manganese . . . . .mg	0.178	0.110	0.096
VITAMINS:			
Ascorbic acid . . . . .mg	55.4	34.3	29.9
Thiamin . . . . .mg	0.063	0.039	0.034
Riboflavin . . . . .mg	0.052	0.032	0.028
Niacin . . . . .mg	0.552	0.342	0.298
Pantothenic acid . . . . .mg	0.122	0.076	0.066
Vitamin B_6 . . . . .mg	0.202	0.125	0.109
Folacin .mcg	51.2	31.7	27.6
Vitamin B_{12} . . . . .mcg	0	0	0
Vitamin A . . . . { RE	1	1	1
{ IU	14	9	8

CELERY, Raw

Nutrients and units	Amount in 100 grams, edible portion	Amount in edible portion of common measures of food	
	Mean	Approximate measure and weight	
		1 stalk = 40 g	½ c dices = 60 g
—————— A ——————	—— B ——	—— E ——	—— F ——
PROXIMATE:			
Water . . . . .g	94.70	37.88	56.82
Food energy . . . . { kcal	16	6	9
{ kj	65	26	39
Protein (N x 6.25) . . . . .g	0.66	0.26	0.40
Total lipid (fat) . . . . .g	0.12	0.05	0.07
Carbohydrate, total . . . . .g	3.63	1.45	2.18
Fiber . . . . .g	0.69	0.28	0.41
Ash . . . . .g	0.89	0.36	0.53
MINERALS:			
Calcium . . . . .mg	36	14	22
Iron . . . . .mg	0.48	0.19	0.29
Magnesium . . . . .mg	12	5	7
Phosphorus . . . . .mg	26	10	16
Potassium . . . . .mg	284	114	170
Sodium . . . . .mg	88	35	53
Zinc . . . . .mg	0.17	0.07	0.10
Copper .mg	0.035	0.014	0.021
Manganese . . . . .mg	0.136	0.054	0.082
VITAMINS:			
Ascorbic acid. . . . . .mg	6.3	2.5	3.8
Thiamin . . . . .mg	0.030	0.012	0.018
Riboflavin . . . . .mg	0.030	0.012	0.018
Niacin. .mg	0.300	0.120	0.180
Pantothenic acid . . . . .mg	0.169	0.068	0.101
Vitamin B_6 . . . . .mg	0.030	0.012	0.018
Folacin . . . . .mcg	8.9	3.6	5.3
Vitamin B_{12} . . . . .mcg	0	0	0
Vitamin A. . . . . { RE	13	5	8
{ IU	127	51	76

CELERY, Cooked, boiled, drained

Nutrients and units	Amount in 100 grams, edible portion	Amount in edible portion of common measures of food	
	Mean	Approximate measure and weight	
		½ c dices = 75 g	1 c dices = 150 g
—————— A ——————	—— B ——	—— E ——	—— F ——
PROXIMATE:			
Water . . . . .g	95.00	71.25	142.50
Food energy . . . . { kcal	15	11	22
{ kj	62	46	92
Protein (N x 6.25) . . . . .g	0.51	0.38	0.76
Total lipid (fat) . . . . .g	0.11	0.08	0.17
Carbohydrate, total . . . . .g	3.52	2.64	5.29
Fiber . . . . .g	0.65	0.49	0.98
Ash . . . . .g	0.86	0.65	1.29
MINERALS:			
Calcium . . . . .mg	36	27	53
Iron . . . . .mg	0.13	0.10	0.20
Magnesium . . . . .mg	12	9	18
Phosphorus . . . . .mg	24	18	36
Potassium . . . . .mg	354	266	531
Sodium . . . . .mg	64	48	97
Zinc . . . . .mg	0.16	0.12	0.23
Copper .mg	0.031	0.023	0.047
Manganese . . . . .mg	0.122	0.092	0.183
VITAMINS:			
Ascorbic acid. . . . . .mg	4.7	3.5	7.1
Thiamin . . . . .mg	0.026	0.020	0.039
Riboflavin . . . . .mg	0.030	0.023	0.045
Niacin. .mg	0.250	0.188	0.375
Pantothenic acid . . . . .mg	0.143	0.107	0.215
Vitamin B_6 . . . . .mg	0.030	0.023	0.045
Folacin . . . . .mcg	6.7	5.0	10.1
Vitamin B_{12} . . . . .mcg	0	0	0
Vitamin A. . . . . { RE	11	8	16
{ IU	108	81	162

CHICORY GREENS, Raw

Nutrients and units	Amount in 100 grams, edible portion	Amount in edible portion of common measures of food	
	Mean	½ c chopped = 90 g	1 c chopped = 180 g
A	B	E	F
PROXIMATE:			
Water . . . . . g	92.00	82.80	165.60
Food energy { kcal	23	21	42
{ kj	98	88	177
Protein (N x 6.25) . . . g	1.70	1.53	3.06
Total lipid (fat) . . . g	0.30	0.27	0.54
Carbohydrate, total . . . g	4.70	4.23	8.46
Fiber . . . . . g	0.80	0.72	1.44
Ash . . . . . g	1.30	1.17	2.34
MINERALS:			
Calcium . . . . . mg	100	90	180
Iron . . . . . mg	0.90	0.81	1.62
Magnesium . . . . . mg	30	27	54
Phosphorus . . . . . mg	47	42	85
Potassium . . . . . mg	420	378	756
Sodium . . . . . mg	45	41	81
Zinc . . . . . mg			
Copper . . . . . mg			
Manganese . . . . . mg			
VITAMINS:			
Ascorbic acid . . . . . mg	24.0	21.6	43.2
Thiamin . . . . . mg	0.060	0.054	0.108
Riboflavin . . . . . mg	0.100	0.090	0.180
Niacin . . . . . mg	0.500	0.450	0.900
Pantothenic acid . . . . . mg			
Vitamin B$_6$ . . . . . mg			
Folacin . . . . . mcg			
Vitamin B$_{12}$ . . . . . mcg	0	0	0
Vitamin A . . . . . { RE	400	360	720
{ IU	4,000	3,600	7,200

COWPEAS, YOUNG PODS WITH SEEDS, Cooked, boiled, drained

Nutrients and units	Amount in 100 grams, edible portion	Amount in edible portion of common measures of food	
	Mean	½ c = 47 g	1 c = 95 g
A	B	E	F
PROXIMATE:			
Water . . . . . g	89.50	42.06	85.02
Food energy { kcal	34	16	32
{ kj	142	67	135
Protein (N x 6.25) . . . g	2.60	1.22	2.47
Total lipid (fat) . . . g	0.30	0.14	0.29
Carbohydrate, total . . . g	7.00	3.29	6.65
Fiber . . . . . g	1.70	0.80	1.62
Ash . . . . . g	0.60	0.28	0.57
MINERALS:			
Calcium . . . . . mg	55	26	52
Iron . . . . . mg	0.70	0.33	0.67
Magnesium . . . . . mg			
Phosphorus . . . . . mg	49	23	47
Potassium . . . . . mg	196	92	186
Sodium . . . . . mg	3	1	3
Zinc . . . . . mg			
Copper . . . . . mg			
Manganese . . . . . mg			
VITAMINS:			
Ascorbic acid . . . . . mg	17.0	8.0	16.2
Thiamin . . . . . mg	0.090	0.042	0.086
Riboflavin . . . . . mg	0.090	0.042	0.086
Niacin . . . . . mg	0.800	0.376	0.760
Pantothenic acid . . . . . mg			
Vitamin B$_6$ . . . . . mg			
Folacin . . . . . mcg			
Vitamin B$_{12}$ . . . . . mcg	0	0	0
Vitamin A . . . . . { RE	140	66	133
{ IU	1,400	658	1,330

CRESS, GARDEN, Raw

Nutrients and units	Amount in 100 grams, edible portion	Amount in edible portion of common measures of food	
	Mean	Approximate measure and weight	
		1 sprig = 1 g	½ c = 25 g
A	B	E	F
PROXIMATE:			
Water . . . . .g	89.40	0.89	22.35
Food energy { kcal	32	0	8
{ kj	134	1	33
Protein (N x 6.25) . . . . .g	2.60	0.03	0.65
Total lipid (fat) . . . . .g	0.70	0.01	0.18
Carbohydrate, total . . . . .g	5.50	0.06	1.38
Fiber . . . . .g	1.10	0.01	0.28
Ash . . . . .g	1.80	0.02	0.45
MINERALS:			
Calcium . . . . .mg	81	1	20
Iron . . . . .mg	1.30	0.01	0.33
Magnesium . . . . .mg			
Phosphorus . . . . .mg	76	1	19
Potassium . . . . .mg	606	6	152
Sodium .mg	14	0	4
Zinc . . . . .mg			
Copper .mg			
Manganese . . . . .mg			
VITAMINS:			
Ascorbic acid . . . . .mg	69.0	0.7	17.3
Thiamin . . . . .mg	0.080	0.001	0.020
Riboflavin . . . . .mg	0.260	0.003	0.065
Niacin . . . . .mg	1.000	0.010	0.250
Pantothenic acid . . . . .mg			
Vitamin B_6 . . . . .mg	0.247	0.002	0.062
Folacin . . . . .mcg			
Vitamin B_{12} . . . . .mcg	0	0	0
Vitamin A . . . . { RE	930	9	233
{ IU	9,300	93	2,325

CUCUMBER, Raw

Nutrients and units	Amount in 100 grams, edible portion	Amount in edible portion of common measures of food	
	Mean	Approximate measure and weight	
		½ c slices = 52 g	1 cucumber = 301 g
A	B	E	F
PROXIMATE:			
Water . . . . .g	96.05	49.94	289.11
Food energy { kcal	13	7	39
{ kj	53	28	160
Protein (N x 6.25) . . . . .g	0.54	0.28	1.63
Total lipid (fat) . . . . .g	0.13	0.07	0.39
Carbohydrate, total . . . . .g	2.91	1.51	8.76
Fiber . . . . .g	0.60	0.31	1.81
Ash . . . . .g	0.38	0.20	1.14
MINERALS:			
Calcium . . . . .mg	14	7	42
Iron . . . . .mg	0.28	0.14	0.84
Magnesium . . . . .mg	11	6	33
Phosphorus . . . . .mg	17	9	51
Potassium . . . . .mg	149	78	448
Sodium .mg	2	1	6
Zinc . . . . .mg	0.23	0.12	0.69
Copper .mg	0.040	0.021	0.120
Manganese . . . . .mg	0.061	0.032	0.184
VITAMINS:			
Ascorbic acid . . . . .mg	4.7	2.4	14.2
Thiamin . . . . .mg	0.030	0.016	0.090
Riboflavin . . . . .mg	0.020	0.010	0.060
Niacin . . . . .mg	0.300	0.156	0.903
Pantothenic acid . . . . .mg	0.250	0.130	0.752
Vitamin B_6 . . . . .mg	0.052	0.027	0.156
Folacin . . . . .mcg	13.9	7.2	41.8
Vitamin B_{12} . . . . .mcg	0	0	0
Vitamin A . . . . { RE	5	2	14
{ IU	45	23	135

GARLIC, Raw

Nutrients and units	Amount in 100 grams, edible portion	Amount in edible portion of common measures of food	
	Mean	Approximate measure and weight	
		1 clove = 3 g	3 cloves = 9 g
A	B	E	F
PROXIMATE:			
Water . . . . .g	58.58	1.76	5.27
Food energy . . . . { kcal	149	4	13
kj	623	19	56
Protein (N x 6.25) . . . . .g	6.36	0.19	0.57
Total lipid (fat) . . . . .g	0.50	0.02	0.05
Carbohydrate, total . . . . .g	33.07	0.99	2.98
Fiber . . . . .g	1.50	0.05	0.14
Ash . . . . .g	1.50	0.05	0.14
MINERALS:			
Calcium . . . . .mg	181	5	16
Iron . . . . .mg	1.70	0.05	0.15
Magnesium . . . . .mg	25	1	2
Phosphorus . . . . .mg	153	5	14
Potassium . . . . .mg	401	12	36
Sodium .mg	17	1	2
Zinc . . . . .mg			
Copper .mg			
Manganese . . . . .mg			
VITAMINS:			
Ascorbic acid . . . . .mg	31.2	0.9	2.8
Thiamin . . . . .mg	0.200	0.006	0.018
Riboflavin . . . . .mg	0.110	0.003	0.010
Niacin . . . . .mg	0.700	0.021	0.063
Pantothenic acid . . . . .mg			
Vitamin B₆ . . . . .mg			
Folacin .mcg	3.1	0.1	0.3
Vitamin B₁₂ . . . . .mcg	0	0	0
Vitamin A . . . . { RE	0	0	0
IU	0	0	0

GINGER ROOT, Raw

Nutrients and units	Amount in 100 grams, edible portion	Amount in edible portion of common measures of food	
	Mean	Approximate measure and weight	
		5 slices = 11 g	¼ c slices = 24 g
A	B	E	F
PROXIMATE:			
Water . . . . .g	81.67	8.98	19.60
Food energy . . . . { kcal	69	8	17
kj	287	34	71
Protein (N x 6.25) . . . . .g	1.74	0.19	0.42
Total lipid (fat) . . . . .g	0.73	0.08	0.18
Carbohydrate, total . . . . .g	15.09	1.66	3.62
Fiber . . . . .g	1.03	0.11	0.25
Ash . . . . .g	0.77	0.08	0.18
MINERALS:			
Calcium . . . . .mg	18	2	4
Iron . . . . .mg	0.50	0.05	0.12
Magnesium . . . . .mg	43	5	10
Phosphorus . . . . .mg	27	3	7
Potassium . . . . .mg	415	46	100
Sodium .mg	13	1	3
Zinc . . . . .mg			
Copper .mg			
Manganese . . . . .mg			
VITAMINS:			
Ascorbic acid . . . . .mg	5.0	0.6	1.2
Thiamin . . . . .mg	0.023	0.003	0.006
Riboflavin . . . . .mg	0.029	0.003	0.007
Niacin . . . . .mg	0.700	0.077	0.168
Pantothenic acid . . . . .mg	0.203	0.022	0.049
Vitamin B₆ . . . . .mg	0.160	0.018	0.038
Folacin .mcg			
Vitamin B₁₂ . . . . .mcg	0	0	0
Vitamin A . . . . { RE	0	0	0
IU	0	0	0

LETTUCE, COS or ROMAINE, Raw

Nutrients and units	Amount in 100 grams, edible portion	Amount in edible portion of common measures of food	
	Mean	Approximate measure and weight	
		1 inner leaf = 10 g	½ c shredded = 28 g
A	B	E	F
PROXIMATE:			
Water . . . . .g	94.91	9.49	26.58
Food energy . . . . { kcal	16	2	4
kj	67	7	19
Protein (N x 6.25) . . . . .g	1.62	0.16	0.45
Total lipid (fat) . . . . .g	0.20	0.02	0.06
Carbohydrate, total . . . . .g	2.37	0.24	0.66
Fiber . . . . .g	0.70	0.07	0.20
Ash . . . . .g	0.90	0.09	0.25
MINERALS:			
Calcium . . . . .mg	36	4	10
Iron .mg	1.10	0.11	0.31
Magnesium . . . . .mg	6	1	2
Phosphorus . . . . .mg	45	5	13
Potassium . . . . .mg	290	29	81
Sodium . . . . .mg	8	1	2
Zinc .mg			
Copper . . . . .mg			
Manganese . . . . .mg			
VITAMINS:			
Ascorbic acid . . . . .mg	24.0	2.4	6.7
Thiamin . . . . .mg	0.100	0.010	0.028
Riboflavin . . . . .mg	0.100	0.010	0.028
Niacin . . . . .mg	0.500	0.050	0.140
Pantothenic acid . . . . .mg			
Vitamin B_6 . . . . .mg			
Folacin . . . . .mcg	135.7	13.6	38.0
Vitamin B_{12} . . . . .mcg	0	0	0
Vitamin A . . . . { RE	260	26	73
IU	2,600	260	728

LETTUCE, ICEBERG, Raw

Nutrients and units	Amount in 100 grams, edible portion	Amount in edible portion of common measures of food	
	Mean	Approximate measure and weight	
		1 leaf = 20 g	1 head = 539 g
A	B	E	F
PROXIMATE:			
Water . . . . .g	95.89	19.18	516.85
Food energy . . . . { kcal	13	3	70
kj	53	11	286
Protein (N x 6.25) . . . . .g	1.01	0.20	5.44
Total lipid (fat) . . . . .g	0.19	0.04	1.02
Carbohydrate, total . . . . .g	2.09	0.42	11.26
Fiber . . . . .g	0.53	0.11	2.86
Ash . . . . .g	0.48	0.10	2.59
MINERALS:			
Calcium . . . . .mg	19	4	102
Iron .mg	0.50	0.10	2.70
Magnesium . . . . .mg	9	2	48
Phosphorus . . . . .mg	20	4	108
Potassium . . . . .mg	158	32	852
Sodium . . . . .mg	9	2	48
Zinc .mg	0.22	0.04	1.19
Copper . . . . .mg	0.028	0.006	0.151
Manganese . . . . .mg	0.151	0.030	0.814
VITAMINS:			
Ascorbic acid . . . . .mg	3.9	0.8	21.0
Thiamin . . . . .mg	0.046	0.009	0.248
Riboflavin . . . . .mg	0.030	0.006	0.162
Niacin . . . . .mg	0.187	0.037	1.008
Pantothenic acid . . . . .mg	0.046	0.009	0.248
Vitamin B_6 . . . . .mg	0.040	0.008	0.216
Folacin . . . . .mcg	56.0	11.2	301.8
Vitamin B_{12} . . . . .mcg	0	0	0
Vitamin A . . . . { RE	33	7	178
IU	330	66	1,779

ONIONS, Raw

Nutrients and units	Amount in 100 grams, edible portion	Amount in edible portion of common measures of food	
	Mean	Approximate measure and weight	
		1 tbsp chopped = 10 g	½ c chopped = 80 g
A	B	E	F
PROXIMATE:			
Water . . . . .g	90.82	9.08	72.65
Food energy { kcal	34	3	27
{ kj	141	14	112
Protein (N x 6.25) . . . . .g	1.18	0.12	0.94
Total lipid (fat) . . . . .g	0.26	0.03	0.21
Carbohydrate, total . . . . .g	7.32	0.73	5.86
Fiber . . . . .g	0.44	0.04	0.35
Ash . . . . .g	0.42	0.04	0.34
MINERALS:			
Calcium . . . . .mg	25	2	20
Iron . . . . .mg	0.37	0.04	0.29
Magnesium . . . . .mg	10	1	8
Phosphorus . . . . .mg	29	3	23
Potassium . . . . .mg	155	16	124
Sodium .mg	2	0	2
Zinc . . . . .mg	0.18	0.02	0.14
Copper .mg	0.040	0.004	0.032
Manganese . . . . .mg	0.133	0.013	0.106
VITAMINS:			
Ascorbic acid . . . . .mg	8.4	0.8	6.7
Thiamin .mg	0.060	0.006	0.048
Riboflavin . . . . .mg	0.010	0.001	0.008
Niacin . . . . .mg	0.100	0.010	0.080
Pantothenic acid . . . . .mg	0.132	0.013	0.106
Vitamin B$_6$ . . . . .mg	0.157	0.016	0.126
Folacin .mcg	19.9	2.0	15.9
Vitamin B$_{12}$ . . . . .mcg	0	0	0
Vitamin A . . . . { RE	0	0	0
{ IU	0	0	0

ONIONS, Cooked, boiled, drained

Nutrients and units	Amount in 100 grams, edible portion	Amount in edible portion of common measures of food	
	Mean	Approximate measure and weight	
		1 tbsp chopped = 15 g	½ c chopped = 105 g
A	B	E	F
PROXIMATE:			
Water . . . . .g	92.24	13.84	96.85
Food energy { kcal	28	4	29
{ kj	117	18	123
Protein (N x 6.25) . . . . .g	0.90	0.14	0.95
Total lipid (fat) . . . . .g	0.16	0.02	0.17
Carbohydrate, total . . . . .g	6.28	0.94	6.59
Fiber . . . . .g	0.42	0.06	0.44
Ash . . . . .g	0.42	0.06	0.44
MINERALS:			
Calcium . . . . .mg	27	4	29
Iron . . . . .mg	0.20	0.03	0.21
Magnesium . . . . .mg	10	2	11
Phosphorus . . . . .mg	23	3	24
Potassium . . . . .mg	152	23	159
Sodium .mg	8	1	8
Zinc . . . . .mg	0.18	0.03	0.19
Copper .mg	0.040	0.006	0.042
Manganese . . . . .mg	0.112	0.017	0.118
VITAMINS:			
Ascorbic acid . . . . .mg	5.7	0.9	6.0
Thiamin .mg	0.042	0.006	0.044
Riboflavin . . . . .mg	0.008	0.001	0.008
Niacin . . . . .mg	0.080	0.012	0.084
Pantothenic acid . . . . .mg	0.127	0.019	0.133
Vitamin B$_6$ . . . . .mg	0.180	0.027	0.189
Folacin .mcg	12.7	1.9	13.3
Vitamin B$_{12}$ . . . . .mcg	0	0	0
Vitamin A . . . . { RE	0	0	0
{ IU	0	0	0

PARSLEY, Raw

Nutrients and units	Amount in 100 grams, edible portion	Amount in edible portion of common measures of food	
	Mean	Approximate measure and weight	
		10 sprigs = 10 g	½ c chopped = 30 g
A	B	E	F
PROXIMATE:			
Water ....g	88.31	8.83	26.49
Food energy ⎰ kcal	33	3	10
⎱ kj	136	14	41
Protein (N x 6.25) ....g	2.20	0.22	0.66
Total lipid (fat) ....g	0.30	0.03	0.09
Carbohydrate, total ....g	6.91	0.69	2.07
Fiber ....g	1.20	0.12	0.36
Ash ....g	2.28	0.23	0.68
MINERALS:			
Calcium ....mg	130	13	39
Iron ....mg	6.20	0.62	1.86
Magnesium ....mg	44	4	13
Phosphorus................mg	41	4	12
Potassium ....mg	536	54	161
Sodium ....mg	39	4	12
Zinc ....mg	0.73	0.07	0.22
Copper ....mg	0.055	0.006	0.017
Manganese ....mg	0.160	0.016	0.048
VITAMINS:			
Ascorbic acid...............mg	90.0	9.0	27.0
Thiamin ....mg	0.080	0.008	0.024
Riboflavin ....mg	0.110	0.011	0.033
Niacin ....mg	0.700	0.070	0.210
Pantothenic acid ....mg	0.300	0.030	0.090
Vitamin B₆................mg	0.164	0.016	0.049
Folacin ....mcg	183.1	18.3	54.9
Vitamin B₁₂ ....mcg	0	0	0
Vitamin A.......... ⎰ RE	520	52	156
⎱ IU	5,200	520	1,560

PARSLEY, Freeze-dried

Nutrients and units	Amount in 100 grams, edible portion	Amount in edible portion of common measures of food	
	Mean	Approximate measure and weight	
		1 tbsp = 0.4 g	¼ c = 1.4 g
A	B	E	F
PROXIMATE:			
Water ....g	2.00	0.01	0.03
Food energy ⎰ kcal	271	1	4
⎱ kj	1,135	5	16
Protein (N x 6.25) ....g	31.30	0.13	0.44
Total lipid (fat) ....g	5.20	0.02	0.07
Carbohydrate, total ....g	42.38	0.17	0.59
Fiber ....g	10.06	0.04	0.14
Ash ....g	19.12	0.08	0.27
MINERALS:			
Calcium ....mg	176	1	2
Iron ....mg	53.90	0.22	0.75
Magnesium ....mg	372	1	5
Phosphorus................mg	548	2	8
Potassium ....mg	6,300	25	88
Sodium ....mg	391	2	5
Zinc ....mg	6.11	0.02	0.09
Copper ....mg	0.459	0.002	0.006
Manganese ....mg	1.338	0.005	0.019
VITAMINS:			
Ascorbic acid...............mg	149.0	0.6	2.1
Thiamin ....mg	1.040	0.004	0.015
Riboflavin ....mg	2.260	0.009	0.032
Niacin ....mg	10.400	0.042	0.146
Pantothenic acid ....mg	2.516	0.010	0.035
Vitamin B₆................mg	1.375	0.006	0.019
Folacin ....mcg	1,535.4	6.1	21.5
Vitamin B₁₂ ....mcg	0	0	0
Vitamin A.......... ⎰ RE	6,324	25	89
⎱ IU	63,240	253	885

PEPPERS, SWEET, Raw

Includes green and red varieties

Nutrients and units	Amount in 100 grams, edible portion	Amount in edible portion of common measures of food	
	Mean	Approximate measure and weight	
		1 pepper = 74 g	½ c chopped = 50 g
A	B	E	F
PROXIMATE:			
Water . . . . .g	92.77	68.65	46.38
Food energy . . . . { kcal	25	18	12
{ kj	104	77	52
Protein (N x 6.25) . . . . .g	0.85	0.63	0.43
Total lipid (fat) . . . . .g	0.45	0.33	0.23
Carbohydrate, total . . . . .g	5.31	3.93	2.66
Fiber . . . . .g	1.20	0.89	0.60
Ash . . . . .g	0.62	0.46	0.31
MINERALS:			
Calcium . . . . .mg	6	4	3
Iron . . . . .mg	1.27	0.94	0.63
Magnesium . . . . .mg	14	10	7
Phosphorus . . . . .mg	22	16	11
Potassium . . . . .mg	195	144	98
Sodium .mg	3	2	2
Zinc . . . . .mg	0.18	0.13	0.09
Copper .mg	0.103	0.076	0.052
Manganese . . . . .mg	0.140	0.104	0.070
VITAMINS:			
Ascorbic acid . . . . .mg	128.0	94.7	64.0
Thiamin . . . . .mg	0.085	0.063	0.043
Riboflavin . . . . .mg	0.050	0 037	0.025
Niacin . . . . .mg	0.550	0.407	0.275
Pantothenic acid . . . . .mg	0.036	0.027	0.018
Vitamin B₆ . . . . .mg	0.164	0.121	0.082
Folacin . . . . .mcg	16.9	12.5	8.4
Vitamin B₁₂ . . . . .mcg	0	0	0
Vitamin A . . . . { RE	53	39	26
{ IU	530	392	265

PEPPERS, SWEET, Cooked, boiled, drained

Includes green and red varieties.

Nutrients and units	Amount in 100 grams, edible portion	Amount in edible portion of common measures of food	
	Mean	Approximate measure and weight	
		1 pepper = 73 g	½ c chopped = 68 g
A	B	E	F
PROXIMATE:			
Water . . . . .g	94.70	69.13	64.40
Food energy . . . . { kcal	18	13	12
{ kj	76	56	52
Protein (N x 6.25) . . . . .g	0.62	0.45	0.42
Total lipid (fat) . . . . .g	0 33	0.24	0.22
Carbohydrate, total . . . . .g	3.89	2.84	2.65
Fiber . . . . .g	0.88	0.64	0.60
Ash . . . . .g	0.45	0.33	0.31
MINERALS:			
Calcium . . . . .mg	4	3	3
Iron . . . . .mg	0.88	0.64	0.60
Magnesium . . . . .mg	10	7	7
Phosphorus . . . . .mg	15	11	10
Potassium . . . . .mg	129	94	88
Sodium .mg	2	2	1
Zinc . . . . .mg	0 12	0.09	0.08
Copper .mg	0.071	0.052	0.048
Manganese . . . . .mg	0.097	0.071	0.066
VITAMINS:			
Ascorbic acid . . . . .mg	111.4	81.3	75.8
Thiamin . . . . .mg	0.053	0.039	0.036
Riboflavin . . . . .mg	0.035	0.026	0.024
Niacin . . . . .mg	0.363	0.265	0.247
Pantothenic acid . . . . .mg	0.023	0.017	0.016
Vitamin B₆ . . . . .mg	0.108	0.079	0.073
Folacin . . . . .mcg	9.9	7.2	6.7
Vitamin B₁₂ . . . . .mcg	0	0	0
Vitamin A . . . . { RE	39	28	26
{ IU	388	283	264

SPINACH, Raw

Nutrients and units	Amount in 100 grams, edible portion	Amount in edible portion of common measures of food	
	Mean	Approximate measure and weight	
		½ c chopped = 28 g	10 oz pkg = 284 g
A	B	E	F
PROXIMATE:			
Water . . . . g	91.58	25.64	186.82
Food energy . . . . { kcal	22	6	46
{ kj	94	26	191
Protein (N x 6.25) . . . . g	2.86	0.80	5.83
Total lipid (fat) . . . . g	0.35	0.10	0.71
Carbohydrate, total . . . . g	3.50	0.98	7.13
Fiber . . . . g	0.89	0.25	1.82
Ash . . . . g	1.72	0.48	3.50
MINERALS:			
Calcium . . . . mg	99	28	202
Iron . . . . mg	2.71	0.76	5.52
Magnesium . . . . mg	79	22	161
Phosphorus . . . . mg	49	14	100
Potassium . . . . mg	558	156	1,139
Sodium . . . . mg	79	22	160
Zinc . . . . mg	0.53	0.15	1.09
Copper . . . . mg	0.130	0.036	0.265
Manganese . . . . mg	0.897	0.251	1.830
VITAMINS:			
Ascorbic acid . . . . mg	28.1	7.9	57.4
Thiamin . . . . mg	0.078	0.022	0.159
Riboflavin . . . . mg	0.189	0.053	0.386
Niacin . . . . mg	0.724	0.203	1.477
Pantothenic acid . . . . mg	0.065	0.018	0.133
Vitamin B_6 . . . . mg	0.195	0.055	0.398
Folacin . . . . mcg	194.4	54.4	396.5
Vitamin B_{12} . . . . mcg	0	0	0
Vitamin A . . . . { RE	672	188	1,370
{ IU	6,715	1,880	13,699

SPINACH, Cooked, boiled, drained

Nutrients and units	Amount in 100 grams, edible portion	Amount in edible portion of common measures of food	
	Mean	Approximate measure and weight	
		½ c = 90 g	1 c = 180 g
A	B	E	F
PROXIMATE:			
Water . . . . g	91.21	82.09	164.18
Food energy . . . . { kcal	23	21	41
{ kj	95	86	172
Protein (N x 6.25) . . . . g	2.97	2.67	5.35
Total lipid (fat) . . . . g	0.26	0.23	0.47
Carbohydrate, total . . . . g	3.75	3.38	6.75
Fiber . . . . g	0.88	0.79	1.59
Ash . . . . g	1.81	1.63	3.26
MINERALS:			
Calcium . . . . mg	136	122	244
Iron . . . . mg	3.57	3.21	6.42
Magnesium . . . . mg	87	79	157
Phosphorus . . . . mg	56	50	100
Potassium . . . . mg	466	419	838
Sodium . . . . mg	70	63	126
Zinc . . . . mg	0.76	0.69	1.37
Copper . . . . mg	0.174	0.157	0.313
Manganese . . . . mg	0.935	0.842	1.683
VITAMINS:			
Ascorbic acid . . . . mg	9.8	8.9	17.7
Thiamin . . . . mg	0.095	0.086	0.171
Riboflavin . . . . mg	0.236	0.212	0.425
Niacin . . . . mg	0.490	0.441	0.882
Pantothenic acid . . . . mg	0.145	0.131	0.261
Vitamin B_6 . . . . mg	0.242	0.218	0.436
Folacin . . . . mcg	145.8	131.2	262.4
Vitamin B_{12} . . . . mcg	0	0	0
Vitamin A . . . . { RE	819	737	1,474
{ IU	8,190	7,371	14,742

TOMATOES, GREEN, Raw

Nutrients and units	Amount in 100 grams, edible portion	Amount in edible portion of common measures of food
	Mean	Approximate measure and weight 1 tomato = 123 g
A	B	E ————— F
PROXIMATE:		
Water . . . . g	93.00	114.39
Food energy . . . . { kcal	24	30
kj	100	124
Protein (N x 6.25) . . . . g	1.20	1.48
Total lipid (fat) . . . . g	0.20	0.25
Carbohydrate, total . . . . g	5.10	6.27
Fiber . . . . g	0.50	0.62
Ash . . . . g	0.50	0.62
MINERALS:		
Calcium . . . . mg	13	16
Iron . . . . mg	0.51	0.63
Magnesium . . . . mg	10	13
Phosphorus . . . . mg	28	35
Potassium . . . . mg	204	251
Sodium . . . . mg	13	16
Zinc . . . . mg	0.07	0.09
Copper . . . . mg	0.090	0.111
Manganese . . . . mg	0.100	0.123
VITAMINS:		
Ascorbic acid . . . . mg	23.4	28.8
Thiamin . . . . mg	0.060	0.074
Riboflavin . . . . mg	0.040	0.049
Niacin . . . . mg	0.500	0.615
Pantothenic acid . . . . mg	0.500	0.615
Vitamin B_6 . . . . mg		
Folacin . . . . mcg		
Vitamin B_{12} . . . . mcg	0	0
Vitamin A . . . . { RE	64	79
IU	642	789

TOMATOES, RED, Ripe, raw

Nutrients and units	Amount in 100 grams, edible portion	Amount in edible portion of common measures of food	
	Mean	Approximate measure and weight	
		1 tomato = 123 g	1 c chopped = 180 g
A	B	E	F
PROXIMATE:			
Water . . . . g	93.95	115.56	169.11
Food energy . . . . { kcal	19	24	35
kj	81	100	146
Protein (N x 6.25) . . . . g	0.89	1.09	1.60
Total lipid (fat) . . . . g	0.21	0.26	0.39
Carbohydrate, total . . . . g	4.34	5.34	7.81
Fiber . . . . g	0.47	0.57	0.84
Ash . . . . g	0.61	0.75	1.10
MINERALS:			
Calcium . . . . mg	7	8	12
Iron . . . . mg	0.48	0.59	0.86
Magnesium . . . . mg	11	14	20
Phosphorus . . . . mg	23	29	42
Potassium . . . . mg	207	254	372
Sodium . . . . mg	8	10	15
Zinc . . . . mg	0.11	0.13	0.19
Copper . . . . mg	0.077	0.095	0.139
Manganese . . . . mg	0.122	0.150	0.220
VITAMINS:			
Ascorbic acid . . . . mg	17.6	21.6	31.6
Thiamin . . . . mg	0.060	0.074	0.108
Riboflavin . . . . mg	0.050	0.062	0.090
Niacin . . . . mg	0.600	0.738	1.080
Pantothenic acid . . . . mg	0.247	0.304	0.445
Vitamin B_6 . . . . mg	0.048	0.059	0.086
Folacin . . . . mcg	9.4	11.5	16.8
Vitamin B_{12} . . . . mcg	0	0	0
Vitamin A . . . . { RE	113	139	204
IU	1,133	1,394	2,039

Index

Healthy Habits

are easy to come by—

IF YOU KNOW WHERE TO LOOK!

Get the latest information on:

- **better health • diet & weight loss**
- **the latest nutritional supplements**
- **herbal healing • homeopathy and more**

COMPLETE AND RETURN THIS CARD RIGHT AWAY!

Where did you purchase this book?

- ❑ bookstore
- ❑ health food store
- ❑ pharmacy
- ❑ supermarket
- ❑ other (please specify)_____

Name_____

Street Address_____

City_____State_____Zip_____

RECEIVE A FREE COPY OF AVERY'S HEALTH CATALOG

GIVE ONE TO A FRIEND ...

Healthy Habits

are easy to come by—

IF YOU KNOW WHERE TO LOOK!

Get the latest information on:

- **better health • diet & weight loss**
- **the latest nutritional supplements**
- **herbal healing • homeopathy and more**

COMPLETE AND RETURN THIS CARD RIGHT AWAY!

Where did you purchase this book?

- ❑ bookstore
- ❑ health food store
- ❑ pharmacy
- ❑ supermarket
- ❑ other (please specify)_____

Name_____

Street Address_____

City_____State_____Zip_____

RECEIVE A FREE COPY OF AVERY'S HEALTH CATALOG

Avery Publishing Group

120 Old Broadway
Garden City Park, NY 11040

Avery Publishing Group

120 Old Broadway
Garden City Park, NY 11040